Competitive Math for Grades 3-8

Samika B. Kulkarni

Thanks to my Mom and Dad for their support

Preface

I'm super-excited to share my new book with you. As a 16-year old High School student, I've been in your shoes giving many competitive Math exams at area, region, and state level.

There is no easy way to master Math. In competitive exams, it is important to keep your poise, be able to perform well under pressure, and solve the problems quickly and correctly.

As I went through this journey, there were a few concepts I learned the hard way, mastered some fast ways of doing problems, and leveraged shortcuts to get to the solutions quickly. Competitive Math always stretches you beyond your actual school grade, as it includes advanced problems.

You will find a variety of problems in this book that deal with topics in Geometry, Algebra, Trigonometry, and Pre-Calculus. I hope that they add to your learning and make you feel more confident as you participate in Math competitions. The problems in this book are inspired by curriculum taught in schools and competitions such as TMSCA, Math Counts, UIL, Olympiad, etc.

Although Math competitions can be stressful and demanding, over the years they have really enhanced my love and appreciation for such analytical subjects. It has also helped to improve my performance in school.

I'm thankful to my parents, teachers, and many other coaches along the way who encouraged me to stretch my boundaries.

I do hope that you benefit from reading this book. Good luck and have fun with Math!

1. If $f(x) = x^3$, $g(x) = \frac{1}{\sqrt{x-244}}$, and $h(x) = 4x^2 -2$, then find

   $f(g(f(h(-2))))$

A. *Note: In a function loop, always start solving from the*
   innermost function.

   Here the innermost function is h(-2).

   We know that, $h(x) = 4x^2 -2$,

   We get h(-2) by substituting x= -2 in the above function.

   So, $h(-2) = 4(-2)^2 -2$

   $= 16 - 2$

   $= 14$

   Thus, $h(-2) = 14 \rightarrow (1)$

   The next innermost function is f(h(-2)), substituting (1),

   we get f(14)

   So, now let us calculate f(14)

   We know that $f(x) = x^3$

   Thus, $f(14) = (14)^3$

   So, $f(14) = 2744 \rightarrow (2)$

   The next innermost function is g(f(h(-2))), substituting

   (2), we get g(2744)

   So, now let us calculate g(2744)

   We know that $g(x) = \frac{1}{\sqrt{x-244}}$

   Thus, $g(2744) = \frac{1}{\sqrt{2744-244}} = \frac{1}{\sqrt{2500}} = \frac{1}{50} \rightarrow (3)$

   Now the last function is f(g(f(h(-2)))), substituting (3), we

   get f(1/50).

   So, now let us calculate f(1/50)

   We know that $f(x) = x^3$

   Thus, $f(1/50) = (1/50)^3$

   $= 1/125000.$

2. What is the area of the annulus if OM = 15 and OL = 17?
   $\pi = 3$.

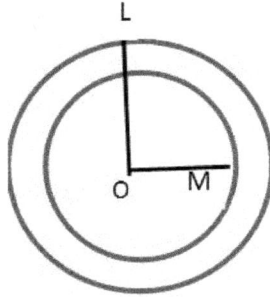

A. *Note:*

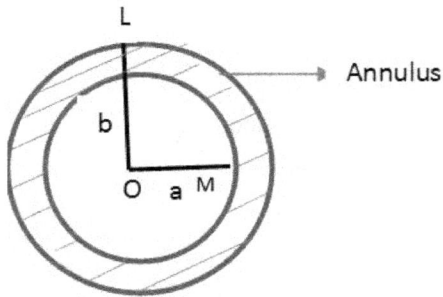

Area of the annulus is $\pi b^2 - \pi a^2$.

Here we have a = 15 and b = 17.

Thus, area of annulus is $\pi(17)^2 - \pi(15)^2$

= 289π - 225π

= 64π

= 64 * 3

=192 sq. units.

3. If 20% of 10% of a is 30, what is $\sqrt{a}$ – a - 20

A. 10% of a = 0.1a

   20% of 10% of a = 0.2 * 0.1a

= 0.02a → (1)

Given 20% of 10% of a is 30

Using (1) we get,

$0.02a = 30$

$a = 1500$ → (2)

Let us use (2) to calculate $\sqrt{a} - a - 20$.

$= \sqrt{1500} - 1500 - 20$

$= \sqrt{100*15} - 1500 - 20$

$= 10\sqrt{15} - 1520$

$= 10(\sqrt{15} - 152)$.

4. MMCD + MDLXVII = _____ (in Arabic form)

A. *Note:*

M=1000

D=500

C=100

L=50

X=10

V=5

I=1

Arabic number is just our regular number system

Operation rules – If the value of a letter is less than the one that follows it, subtract the smaller value from the greater value. This only works when the greater value is within ten times of the smaller value e.g. I & X; C &D.

MM	CD	+	MD	LX	VIII

= 1000+1000 500-100   1000+500   50+10   5+1+1+1

= 2000 + 400 + 1500 + 60 + 8

= 3,968.

5. How many lines of symmetry can be drawn through a regular septagon?

A. *Note: A regular polygon of n sides has n lines of symmetry.*

Thus, a regular septagon that has 7 sides will have 7 lines of symmetry.

6. Solve $|i^2 -8i -7 - 4i|$

A. *Formula:* $|a + bi| = \sqrt{a^2 + b^2}$ *and* $i^2 = -1$

Thus, $|i^2 -8i -7 - 4i|$

$= |-1 - 8i -7 - 4i|$

$= |-8 - 12i|$

Here a = -8 and b = -12.

$= |-8 - 4i| = \sqrt{(-8)^2 + (-12)^2}$

$= \sqrt{208}$

$= 4\sqrt{13}.$

7. Find the determinant of the matrix $\begin{bmatrix} 7 & -11 \\ -2 & -6 \end{bmatrix}$

A. For Matrix $\begin{bmatrix} a & b \\ c & d \end{bmatrix}$

Determinant $|D|$ = ad-bc

Here we have, a =7, b = -11, c =-2 and d= -6

Thus, $|D|$ = ad-bc = 7*(-6) – ((-11)*(-2))

= -42-22

= -64.

8. A tanker holding 50,000 gallons of water develops a leak that spills out 20 gallons/min. After the leak was found out and fixed, there was 15,000 gallons of water left in the tanker. How long in hours did it take to find out and fix

the leak (assume the fix happens immediately after detection)?

A. The water left in the tanker is 15,000 gallons.

So, it spilled out

$50000 - 15000 = 35000$ gallons of water.

The leak spills out 20 gallons/min.

So, to spill out 35000 gallons, it will take

$$= \frac{35000}{20}$$

$= 1750$ min

Let us convert this to hours

$$= \frac{1750}{60}$$

$= \sim29.2$ hours.

9. A baker made 20 baker's dozen of donuts for a party and then increased them by a gross. However, he still fell short by a dozen donuts. How many total donuts did he need?

A. *Note: 1 baker's dozen = 13.*

1 gross = a dozen dozens.

Thus, 20 baker's dozen $= 20 * 13 = 260$ and,

1 gross $= 12 * 12 = 144$

So, the baker made

$= 260 + 144$

$= 404$ donuts

However, he still fell short by a dozen donuts.

So, the total donuts he needed to make were

$= 404 + 12$

$= 416$ donuts.

10. What is the balance on $1000 at annual compound interest rate of 0.6% at the end of 24 months?

A. *Note: Annual Interest, I = P * r * t*

    where, P is Principal, r is annual rate of interest, and t is period in years

    Here, P=$1000.

    r = 0.6/100 = 0.006

    t = 1 year

    Thus, annual interest at the end of year 1 is,

    = 1000 * 0.006 * 1

    = $6

    Since this is a compound interest problem, the balance in the account at the end of year 1 is,

    = 1000 + 6

    = $1006

    Now we need to find out the interest for the balance over the remaining 12 months

    So, we have,

    P = 1006,

    r = 0.006 and

    t = 12 months = 1 year

    Thus, interest over the remaining 12 months

    = 1006 * 0.006 * 1

    = $6.036

    This the total balance in the account at the end of 24 months is,

    = 1006 + 6.036

    = $1,012.04.

    OR another method:

Formula: Compound amount = Principal $(1 + r)^t$

Where, r = rate of interest, and t is the period in years

Here, P=$1000.

r = 0.6/100 = 0.006

t = 24 months = 2 years

Compound amount = 1000 $(1 + 0.006)^2$

= $1,012.04

11. $\dfrac{\dfrac{(3^3 * 4)}{12} - 7 + 24 / 2^2}{-2 - 6 * 4}$

A: *The rules for order of operations are:*

a) *Parenthesis*

b) *Powers*

c) *Multiplication and division from left to right*

d) *Addition and subtraction from left to right*

$\dfrac{\dfrac{(3^3 * 4)}{12} - 7 + 24 / 2^2}{-2 - 6 * 4}$

$= \dfrac{\dfrac{(27 * 4)}{12} - 7 + 24/4}{-2 - 6 * 4}$

$= \dfrac{\dfrac{(108)}{12} - 7 + 24/4}{-2 - 6 * 4}$

$= \dfrac{9 - 7 + 6}{-2 - 24}$

$= \dfrac{8}{-26}$

$= -\dfrac{4}{13}.$

12. 95+96-97+98-99+100-101+102-103+104

A. Rather than adding and subtracting all these numbers, a quick glance reveals a pattern, that can help perform this calculation quickly. Take a look at the underlined pattern,

95+96 -97+98   -99+100 -101+102 -103+104

$= 191 + 1 + 1 + 1 + 1$

$= 195.$

13. What is the sum of the total number of diagonals of both a pentagon and an octagon?

A. *Note: The number of a diagonals of a n-sided polygon is* $\frac{n(n-3)}{2}$.

Thus, the total number of diagonals of a pentagon (n=5) are, $\frac{5(5-3)}{2} = 5 \rightarrow (1)$

And, the total number of diagonals of a octagon (n=8) are, $\frac{8(8-3)}{2} = 20 \rightarrow (2)$

Thus, sum of the total number of diagonals of both a hexagon and a pentagon can be obtained by adding (1) and (2).

=5+20

=25.

14. A $=2x^2 - 9x + 26$ and B $= -x^2 - 10x + 10$, simplify A $- 2B$?

A. A-2B $=$

$(2x^2 - 9x + 26) - 2 (-x^2 - 10x + 10)$

$= 2x^2 - 9x + 26 + 2x^2 + 20x - 20$

$= 4x^2 + 11x + 6$

$= 4x^2 + 8x + 3x + 6$

$= 4x(x + 2) + 3(x + 2)$

$= (4x + 3)(x + 2).$

15. Find the perimeter of an equilateral triangle with a side of $2\sqrt{8}$ - 4?

A. *Note: Perimeter of a n-sided figure, is the sum of its sides.*

Thus, the perimeter of the equilateral triangle (all sides are of the same length) is,

$= 3 * (2\sqrt{8} - 4)$

$= 6\sqrt{8} - 12$

$= 6\sqrt{4*2} - 12$

$= 12\sqrt{2} - 12$

$= 12(\sqrt{2} - 1)$ units.

16. If the side of a right triangle is 9 cm and hypotenuse is 41 cm, what is the length of the remaining side?

A. *Note: Pythagoras theorem of a right triangle states that the sum of the squares of the lengths of the sides of a right triangle is equal to the square of its hypotenuse.*

Thus, we have, (length of hypotenuse)^2 = (length of side 1)^2 + (length of side 2)^2

$(41)^2 = (9)^2 +$ (length of side 2)^2

$1681 = 81 +$ (length of side 2)^2

(length of side 2)$^2 = 1600$

Thus, length of side $= \sqrt{1600} = 40$ cm.

17. If the length of the side of a square is three times the diameter of a circle, what is the radius of the circle if the side of the square is 48?

A: Let s be the length of the square and r the radius of the circle.

We know that diameter $= 2*$ radius $= 2r \rightarrow (1)$

Given that side of the square is three times the diameter of the circle.

So, $s= 3*$ diameter; substituting (1)

$s = 3*2r = 6r \rightarrow (2)$

Given that $s = 48$, substituting in (2)

$6r = 48$

$r = 8$ units.

18. What is the sum of the interior angle of a rectangle and a regular pentagon?

A: *Note: The interior angle of a regular polygon of n-sides is, ((n-2) * 180)/n.*

For a pentagon, $n=5$

Thus, the interior angle is,

$$= \frac{(5-2)*180}{5}$$

$=108° \rightarrow (1)$

The interior angle of a rectangle is $90° \rightarrow (2)$

This the sum of an interior angle of pentagon and rectangle is the sum of (1) and (2)

$= 108 + 90$

$= 198°$.

19. What is the largest power of 3 that divides $3^7 + 3$?

A: Let us try to find least common multiples of $(3^7 + 3)$ in terms of 3, until you can't divide by 3.

$3^7 + 3$

$= 3(3^6 + 1)$

Thus, the largest power of 3 that divides $(3^7 + 3)$ is 3, as $(3^6 + 1)$ cannot be further divided by 3.

20. What is the next number in the sequence $\frac{5}{2}$, 2, $\frac{3}{2}$, 1, __?

A: Let us try to identify the pattern between these numbers.

Let us see if this is an arithmetic series with a fixed difference between consecutive numbers.

Taking the first two numbers, the difference is

$$= 2 - \frac{5}{2} = -\frac{1}{2}$$

If you notice, if we add -1/2 to any number in the above sequence, you get the following number –for example,

$$2 - \frac{1}{2} = \frac{3}{2} \text{ or } \frac{3}{2} - \frac{1}{2} = 1$$

Thus, the next number in the sequence is,

$$= 1 - \frac{1}{2} = \frac{1}{2}.$$

21. $108° = $ ___ radians?

A: *Note: $1° = \pi/180$ radians.*

Thus, $108°$ is,

$$= 108 * \frac{\pi}{180}$$

$$= \frac{3\pi}{5} \text{ radians.}$$

22. Solve the equation $x + \frac{3!}{4} + \frac{1}{2} = \frac{1}{3!}x - \frac{17}{4}$

A:

$$x + \frac{3!}{4} + \frac{1}{2} = \frac{1}{3!}x - \frac{17}{4}$$

$$x + \frac{3 * 2 * 1}{4} + \frac{1}{2} = \frac{1}{3 * 2 * 1}x - \frac{17}{4}$$

$$x + \frac{3}{2} + \frac{1}{2} = \frac{x}{6} - \frac{17}{4}$$

$$x + 2 = \frac{x}{6} - \frac{17}{4}$$

$$x + 2 = \frac{2x - 51}{12}$$

$$12x + 24 = 2x - 51$$

$$10x = -75$$

$$x = -\frac{15}{2}.$$

23. $53_{10} = K_6$ and $27_{10} = M_6$, then $K_6 + M_6$? (Base 6)

A: $K_6 = 53_{10} = 53$

$M_6 = 27_{10} = 27$, then

$K_6 + M_6 = 53 + 27 = 80_{10}$

Let us now convert 80_{10} to base 6.

Step 1 – Divide 80 by 6 (as we are converting to base 6)

$$\begin{array}{r} 13 \\ 6\overline{)80} \\ \underline{-78} \\ 2 \end{array}$$

Make a note of the remainder = 2 → (1)

Step 2 – Divide the quotient from step 1 by 6

$$\begin{array}{r} 2 \\ 6\overline{)13} \\ \underline{-12} \\ 1 \end{array}$$

Make a note of the remainder = 1 → (2)

Step 3 – Divide quotient from step 2 by 6

$6\overline{)2}$

You can't divide 2 by 6, so the remainder of this step is 2 → (3)

Step 4 – Now let us collate the remainders from the above steps, starting with the last step

Using (3), (2) and (1) above we get,

So, we have, 212

Thus, $K_6 + M_6 = 80_{10} = 212_6$.

24. Solve $(3x - 5)^2 + (x - 9)^3$

A: $(3x - 5)^2 + (x - 9)^3$

Note: $(a - b)^2 = a^2 - 2ab + b^2$

Here a = 3x and b = 5, so we have

$$(3x - 5)^2 = (3x)^2 - 2(3x)(5) + (5)^2$$

$= 9x^2 - 30x + 25 \rightarrow (1)$

Note: $(a - b)^3 = a^3 - 3a^2b + 3ab^2 - b^3$

Here $a = x$ and $b = 9$, so we have

$(x - 9)^3 = x^3 - 3x(9)^2 + 3x^2(9) - (9)^3$

$= x^3 - 243x + 27x^2 - 729 \rightarrow (2)$

Thus, using (1) and (2) we get $(3x - 5)^2 + (x - 9)^3$

$= 9x^2 - 30x + 25 + (x^3 - 243x + 27x^2 - 729)$

$= x^3 - 273x + 36x^2 - 704.$

25. $\frac{1}{3} ft^3 = $ ___ $inch^3$?

A: *Note: 1 cubic feet = 1728 cubic inches.*

Thus, $\frac{1}{3} ft^3 = \frac{1}{3} * 1728 = 576 \ in^3$

26. If $(-7^2 + 4)^2 - (-7^2 - 4)^2$

A: Let $a = -7^2$, $b = 4 \rightarrow (1)$

Then, we have, $(a + b)^2 - (a - b)^2$

$= (a^2 + 2ab + b^2) - (a^2 - 2ab + b^2)$

$= 4ab \rightarrow (2)$

Substituting (1) in (2)

$= 4*(-7^2)*(4)$

$= -784.$

27. -127 is what term of the sequence -19, -23, -27, -31,...?

A: *Note: An arithmetic pattern follows the formula:*

$a_n = a_1 + (n - 1)d$

where,

a_1 *is the first term in the sequence*

a_n *is the nth term in the sequence*

d is the difference between two consecutive numbers in the pattern.

Here $a_1 = -19$

$a_n = -127$

$d = -23 - (-19) = -4$

Substituting in the formula, we get:

$-127 = -19 + (n-1)(-4)$

$-127 = -19 - 4n + 4$

$-127 = -4n - 15$

$4n = 112$

$n = 28$

Thus, -127 is the 28th term in the sequence.

28. If there are four consecutive even numbers and the product of the first and third number is twelve less than product of the first and fourth number, then find the product of the second and fourth number?

A: We will assume that the four consecutive even integers are 2n, 2n+2, 2n+4 and 2n+6.

Given, the product of the first and third number is twelve less than product of the first and fourth number.

So, we have,

$2n * (2n + 4) = 2n * (2n + 6) - 12$

$4n^2 + 8n = 4n^2 + 12n - 12$

$4n = 12$

$n = 3$

Thus, the four consecutive numbers are 6,8,10 and 12.

So, the product of second and fourth number is 8*12 = 96.

29. Given a circle whose center is O if the measure of $\angle AOB$ = 129°, what is the measure of arc ACB?

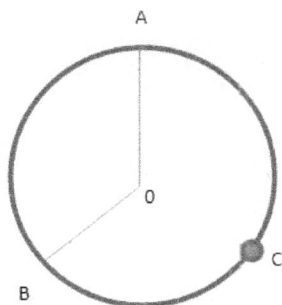

A: *Note: $m(\overarc{AB}) = m\angle AOB$*

Given $m\angle AOB = 129°$

Thus, $m(\overarc{AB}) = 129°$

So, $m(\overarc{ACB}) = 360° - 129°$

$= 231°$.

30. $\left(\left(\sqrt[5]{243}\right)^2 - \sqrt[3]{343}\right)^2$

A: $\left(\left(\sqrt[5]{243}\right)^2 - \sqrt[3]{343}\right)^2$

$= \left(\left(\sqrt[5]{3^5}\right)^2 - \sqrt[3]{7^3}\right)^2$

$= \left((3)^2 - 7\right)^2$

$= (9-7)^2$

$= 4$.

31. A mass of 21g and 30g are on the ends of a meter stick. How far does the fulcrum have to be placed from the 21g mass to balance the meter stick?

A: The given information in the problem can be represented by the following figure:

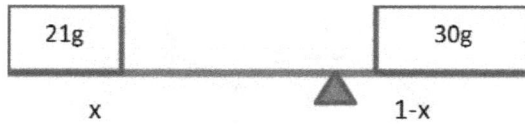

For the fulcrum to balance on a meter stick (1 meter in length), we need to have,

$21x = 30(1 - x)$

$21x = 30 - 30x$

$51x = 30$

$x = 0.59m$

Thus, the fulcrum has to be placed 0.59m from the 21g mass to balance the meter stick.

32. If the discriminant of a quadratic equation is zero, how many real solutions does the quadratic equation have?

A. For a quadratic equation $ax^2 + bx + c = 0$

Discriminant $D = b^2 - 4ac$

If D<0, then there are no real solutions or roots of the equation.

If D>0, then there are two real solutions or roots of the equation.

If D=0, then there is only one real solution or root of the equation.

Here we have discriminant as zero, so there will be one real solution or root.

33. 4 coins are flipped, what is the probability of at least three heads?

A. When a coin is tossed there are two outcomes – head or tail.

With 4 coin tosses there are

2*2*2*2

= 16 outcomes → (1)

When you flip 4 coins and need at least three heads, the permutation of that happening is

{HHHT, HHHH, HTHH, HHTH, THHH}

= 5 outcomes → (2)

Thus, the probability of getting at least three heads in 4 coin flips is obtained by dividing (2) by (1)

$$= \frac{5}{16}.$$

34. Carl's account balance dropped from $1500 to $975, what was the change in percentage?

A.   ((975 - 1500)/1500) * 100

= (-7/20)*100

= -35%

Thus, Carl's account balance dropped by 35%.

35. Find the area of the triangle formed by the x-axis, y-axis and the line y=-3x+6?

A.   The line y=-3x+6 has a negative slope, so visually the question looks like the following:

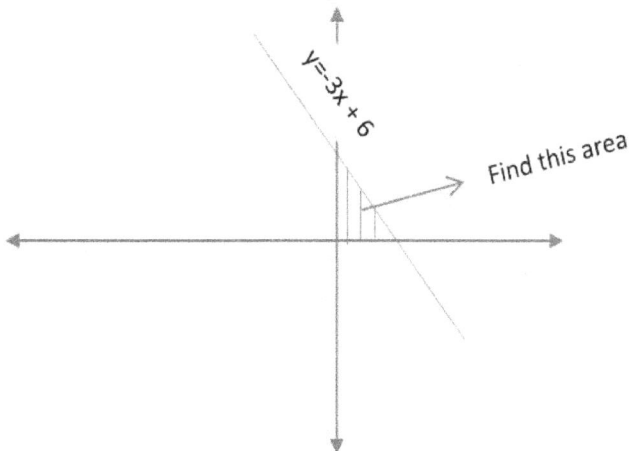

Let us find where the line y=-3x+6 intersects the x-axis:

To find the x-intercept, put y = 0 in the above equation:

y = -3x + 6

0 = -3x + 6

x = 2 → (1)

Thus, the line y=-3x+6 intersects x-axis at (2,0)

Similarly, let us find where the line y=-3x+6 intersects the y-axis:

To find the y-intercept, put x = 0 in the above equation:

y = 0 + 6

y = 6 → (2)

Thus, the line y=-3x+6 intersects y-axis at (0,6).

So, in the above figure, if you look at the shaded triangle that is formed from the intersection of x-axis, y-axis and line y=-3x+6 you'll notice that the triangle has a height of 6 (from (2)) and base of 2 (from (1)).

Thus, area of this triangle is $\frac{1}{2}$ *base* * *height*

$$= \frac{1}{2} * 2 * 6$$

$$= 6 \text{ sq. units.}$$

36. What is the 8th hexagonal number?

A. *Formula: nth hexagonal number is n(2n -1).*

Thus, the 8th hexagonal number is

= 8(2*8 -1)

= 120.

37. Jingle is a smart cat who eats $1/8^{th}$ of a can of her cat food at a time. She eats 4 times a day. How many cans of food do you need to buy for her for a week? Round off to nearest integer.

A. Given that Jingle eats $\frac{1}{8}$th of can at a time.

She eats 4 times a day, so she consumes

$$\frac{1}{8} * 4$$

$$= \frac{1}{2} \text{ can of food a day.}$$

So, for 7 days, we would need to buy

$$\frac{1}{2} * 7 = 3.5 \text{ cans of food.}$$

Rounding off we get, 4 cans.

So, we would need to buy 4 cans of food for Jingle for a week.

38. Simplify $((\frac{27}{125})^{\frac{4}{3}})^2$

A.

$$((\frac{27}{125})^{\frac{4}{3}})^2$$

$$= (\frac{27}{125})^{\frac{8}{3}}$$

$$= (\frac{3^3}{5^3})^{\frac{8}{3}}$$

$$= \frac{(3^3)^{\frac{8}{3}}}{(5^3)^{\frac{8}{3}}}$$

$$= \frac{3^8}{5^8}$$

$$= \frac{6561}{390625}.$$

39. John was 20 years younger than three times Sara's age 8 years ago. Their ages combined now equal 116 years. What is John's current age?

A. Let John's present age be J and Sara's present age be S.

Given, John's and Sara's ages total 116.

J + S = 116 → (1)

Eight years ago, John's age was J-8 and Sara's age was S-8.

Given, John was 20 years younger than three times Sara's age 8 years ago

J - 8 = 3(S - 8) - 20

J - 8 = 3S – 24 - 20

J – 8 = 3S - 44

J - 3S = - 36 → (2)

Subtract (2) from (1)

4S = 152

S = 38 → (3)

Substituting (3) in (1), we get

J + 38 = 116

J = 78

Thus, John's current age is 78 years.

40. What is the area of the triangle in the following figure?

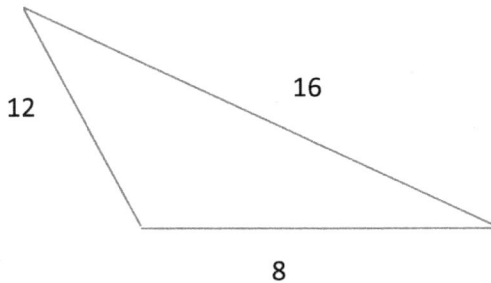

A. *Formula: Area of a triangle where three sides are a, b, and c is:*

$$A = \sqrt{s(s - a)(s - b)(s - c)}$$

where,

$s = \frac{a+b+c}{2}$.

Given, a = 12, b = 8, and c= 16.

Thus, $s = \frac{12+8+16}{2}$

s = 18

So, area of the triangle,

$A = \sqrt{18(18-12)(18-8)(18-16)}$

$= \sqrt{18(6)(10)(2)}$

$= \sqrt{2*9*3*2*2*5*2}$

$= 12\sqrt{15}$ unit^2.

41. Simplify $\sqrt{a^3 - 2a^2 + a} + \sqrt{3a^2 - 3}$

A. $\sqrt{a(a^2 - 2a + 1)} + \sqrt{3(a^2 - 1)}$

$= \sqrt{a(a-1)^2} + \sqrt{3(a+1)(a-1)}$

$= (a-1)\sqrt{a} + \sqrt{3(a+1)(a-1)}$

$= \sqrt{a-1}(\sqrt{a(a-1)} + \sqrt{3(a+1)})$.

42. If 7x-2y =25 and 2x –7y =11; what is the value of x+y?

A. 7x –2y = 25 → (1)

2x –7y = 11 → (2)

Multiply (1) by 2 and multiply (2) by 7

(1) * 2 is: 14x – 4y = 50 → (3)

(2) * 7 is: 14x – 49y = 77 → (4)

Subtract (4) from (3)

45y = -27

$y = -\frac{3}{5}$

Substituting value of y in (1) we get,

7x -2$(-\frac{3}{5})$ = 25

$$7x + \left(\frac{6}{5}\right) = 25$$

$$35x = 119$$

$$x = \frac{17}{5}$$

Thus, x + y

$$= \frac{17}{5} - \frac{3}{5}$$

$$= \frac{14}{5}.$$

43. What is the arithmetic mean of 2^3, -5^2, $(-6)^3$?

A. $2^3 = 8$

$-5^2 = -25$

$(-6)^3 = -216$

Arithmetic mean of the above 3 numbers is,

$$= \frac{8 - 25 - 216}{3}$$

$$= -\frac{233}{3}$$

$$= -77.66.$$

44. How many 6-digit license plates can be formed using the digits 1 through 9 (inclusive) when digits cannot be repeated?

A. The set is (1, 2, 3, 4, 5, 6, 7, 8, 9) = 9 digits

Note: The number of r digit license plates using these n digits, without any repetition, is obtained using Permutation.

$$^nP_r = \frac{n!}{(n-r)!}$$

Here, n = 9 and r = 6, so we get:

$$^7P_5 = \frac{9!}{(9-6)!}$$

$$= \frac{9*8*7*6*5*4*3*2*1}{3*2*1}$$

$= 60,480.$

45. What is the additive inverse of the opposite of the reciprocal of the slope of the line perpendicular to the line $3x - 7y = 9$?

A. *Note: The slope-intercept form of the line is y=mx+ b; where m is the slope.*

Here the equation of the line is $3x - 7y = 9$.

Rearranging to get to the standard slope-intercept form:

$7y = 3x - 9$

$$y = \frac{3}{7}x - \frac{9}{7}$$

Comparing to the standard slope-intercept form of the line, we have slope $= \frac{3}{7}$.

The slope of the line perpendicular to the above line is $-\frac{7}{3}$

Note: The product of a number and its reciprocal is one.

The reciprocal of the slope of the perpendicular line is $-\frac{3}{7}$.

The opposite of the reciprocal is $+\frac{3}{7}$.

Note: The sum of a number and its additive inverse is zero.

Thus, the additive inverse of the opposite is $-\frac{3}{7}$.

46. If M and N are integers and $N = M - 1$, then what is $\frac{(M+2)!}{N!}$?

A. Given $N = M - 1$

We have to calculate $\frac{(M+2)!}{N!} = \frac{(M+2)!}{(M-1)!}$

Note: A! = A(A-1)(A-2)...1

So, we have,

$$= \frac{(M+2)(M+1)M(M-1)!}{(M-1)!}$$

$$= M(M+1)(M+2).$$

47. $\frac{5x^2-x-6}{4x^2-11x+6} \div (x+1)$

A. $\frac{5x^2-x-6}{4x^2-11x+6} \div (x+1)$

Factoring the equations:

$$= \frac{5x^2+5x-6x-6}{4x^2-8x-3x+6} \div (x+1)$$

$$= \frac{5x(x+1)-6(x+1)}{4x(x-2)-3(x-2)} \div (x+1)$$

$$= \frac{(5x-6)(x+1)}{(4x-3)(x-2)} \div (x+1)$$

$$= \frac{(5x-6)(x+1)}{(4x-3)(x-2)(x+1)}$$

$$= \frac{(5x-6)}{(4x-3)(x-2)}.$$

48. Solve the equation $|3x-6| = 2x+9$

A. Note: $|A| = \pm A$

$3x - 6 = \pm (2x+9)$

Solving for x we have two values:

1. $3x - 6 = + (2x+9)$

    $x = 15$

2. $3x - 6 = - (2x+9)$

    $3x - 6 = -2x - 9$

    $5x = -3$

    $x = -\frac{3}{5}$

Since the equation has a modulus sign, the answer needs to be positive, so we choose the positive value out of the two values of x above.

Thus, x = 15.

49. What is the area of the ellipse? π = 3.

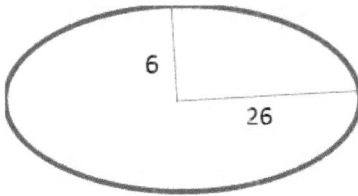

A. Note: The area of an ellipse is π * r_1 * r_2, where r_1 and r_2 are radii of the ellipse

Here, π = 3, r_1 = 6, and r_2 = 26.

Thus, area of the ellipse = 3 * 6 * 26 = 468 unit².

50. Find the supplement of ∢NMO, if ∢LMO = $4x^2 + 9x - 27$ and ∢LMN = $3x^3 + x^2 - 2x - 21$

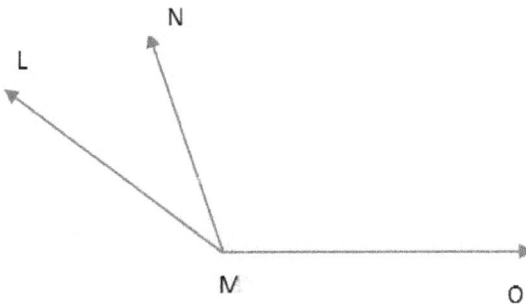

A. $\angle NMO = \angle LMO - \angle LMN$

$= 4x^2 + 9x - 27 - (3x^3 + x^2 - 2x - 21)$

$= 4x^2 + 9x - 27 - 3x^3 - x^2 + 2x + 21$

$= -3x^3 + 3x^2 + 11x - 6$

The supplement of an angle is obtained by subtracting the measure of that angle from 180.

So, we have the supplement of $\angle NMO$

$= 180 - (-3x^3 + 3x^2 + 11x - 6)$

$= 3x^3 - 3x^2 - 11x + 186.$

51. $(4i^4 - 7i^3 - 12) + (2i^2 - 4i)^2$

A.   *Note: $i^2 = -1$ and $i^3 = -i$*

Thus, $(4i^4 - 7i^3 - 12) + (2i^2 - 4i)^2$

$= (4(-1)(-1) - 7(-i) - 12) + (2(-1)-4i)^2$

$= (7i - 8) + (-2 - 4i)^2$

$= 7i - 8 + ((-2)^2 - 2(-2)(4i) + (4i)^2)$

$= 7i - 8 + (4 + 16i + 16i^2)$

$= 7i - 8 + 4 + 16i + 16(-1)$

$= 23i - 20.$

52. What is the equation of a perpendicular bisector of the segment with end points (2,-6) and (-8,-4)?

A.   We need to know the slope of the bisector and a point on the bisector segment in order to define its equation.

Note: Midpoint of a segment with end points (x_1, y_1) and (x_2, y_2) is:

x *co-ordinate* $= \dfrac{x_1 + x_2}{2}$ *and*

y *co-ordinate* $= \dfrac{y_1 + y_2}{2}$

Let us first find the po.nt on the bisector, which is the midpoint of the segment with endpoints (2, -6) and (-8, -4)

x co-ordinate = $\dfrac{2-8}{2}$ = -3

y co-ordinate = $\dfrac{-6-4}{2}$ = -5

The point (-3, -5) will be on the bisector.

Now let us find the slope of the perpendicular bisector. To do this, first let us finc the slope of the segment with end points (2, -6) and (-8, -4).

Note: Slope of a segment with end points (x_1, y_1) and (x_2, y_2) is:

$\dfrac{y_1 - y_2}{x_1 - x_2}$

The slope of the line with (2, -6) and (-8, -4) is:

$= \dfrac{-6-(-4)}{2-(-8)}$

$= -\dfrac{1}{5}$

The product of the slopes of two perpendicular lines is -1. Thus, the slope of the perpendicular that bisects the segment with end points (2, -6) and (-8, -4) will be 5.

Using the point-slope form of line equation $(y - y_1) = m(x - x_1)$, the equation of the bisector with point (-3, -5) and slope 5 is

$y - (-5) = 5(x - (-3))$

$y + 5 = 5(x + 3)$

$y = 5x + 10$.

53. Two cars are traveling in the same direction at speeds of 45 mph and 60 mph. The faster car leaves the starting

point two hours after the first car. How far from the starting point will the two cars pass each other?

A. Let Car 1 be the car with speed of 45 mph and Car 2 be the car with speed of 60 mph.

Let us assume that the cars meet at distance d from the starting point. Let us assume it takes Car 1 t hours to travel the distance d.

We know that distance = speed * time

So for Car 1 we have,

$d = 45t$ → (1)

We know that Car 2 leaves the starting point two hours after Car 1, so it will take Car 2 $(t - 2)$ hours to travel the distance d.

So, for Car 2 we have,

$d = 60(t - 2)$ → (2)

Comparing (1) and (2) we get,

$45t = 60(t-2)$

$45t = 60t - 120$

$15t = 120$

$t = 8$ hours

Thus, the two cars will meet after 8 hours.

To find out the distance at which they will meet from the starting point, we substitute the value of t in (1), we get,

$= 45 * 8$

$= 360$ miles.

54. $(55 * 10^{-6})(400,000,000)$

A. $(55 * 10^{-6})(400,000,000)$

Let's convert this to exponential format to make it easier.

$= (5.5 * 10 * 10^{-6})(4 * 10^8)$

$= (5.5 * 10^{-5}) (4 * 10^8)$

Rearranging we get,

$= (5.5 * 4) (10^{-5} * 10^8)$

$= 22 * 10^3$

$= 2.2 * 10 * 10^3$

$= 2.2 * 10^4.$

55. $-45^2 + (-3 + 16)^2$

A. *Note: There is a difference between $-n^2$ and $(-n)^2$; the former is $-n^2$ while the latter is n^2.*

$-45^2 + (-3 - 16)^2$

$= -2025 + (-19)^2$

$= -2025 + 361$

$= -1664.$

56. If the inner diagonal of a prism is $7\sqrt{5}$ cm and the length and width are 6 cm, and 7 cm, find the height of the prism

A. *Inner diagonal of a prism* $= \sqrt{l^2 + w^2 + h^2}$

$7\sqrt{5} = \sqrt{6^2 + 7^2 + h^2}$

Squaring both sides we get,

$245 = 6^2 + 7^2 + h^2$

$245 = 36 + 49 + h^2$

$h^2 + 85 = 245$

$h^2 = 160$

$h = 4\sqrt{10}$ cm.

57. Find the inverse of the matrix of the product of:

$$-\frac{1}{4} \cdot \begin{bmatrix} -4 & -2 \\ 3 & -5 \end{bmatrix} \cdot \begin{bmatrix} 3 & -5 \\ 4 & -5 \end{bmatrix}$$

A. *Formula for* $\begin{bmatrix} a & b \\ c & d \end{bmatrix} \cdot \begin{bmatrix} e & f \\ g & h \end{bmatrix} = \begin{bmatrix} ae + bg & af + bh \\ ce + dg & cf + dh \end{bmatrix}$

$$-\frac{1}{4} \cdot \begin{bmatrix} -4 & -2 \\ 3 & -5 \end{bmatrix} \cdot \begin{bmatrix} 3 & -5 \\ 4 & -5 \end{bmatrix}$$

$$= -\frac{1}{4} \cdot \begin{bmatrix} (-4*3)+(-2*4) & (-4*-5)+(-2*-5) \\ 3*3+(-5*4) & (3*-5)+(-5*-5) \end{bmatrix}$$

$$= -\frac{1}{4} \cdot \begin{bmatrix} -20 & 30 \\ -11 & 10 \end{bmatrix}$$

Note: $k. \begin{bmatrix} a & b \\ c & d \end{bmatrix} = \begin{bmatrix} ka & kb \\ kc & kd \end{bmatrix}$

$$= \begin{bmatrix} 5 & -7.5 \\ 2.75 & -2.5 \end{bmatrix}$$

Determinant of $\begin{bmatrix} a & b \\ c & d \end{bmatrix}$ *is ad-bc*

Here a = 5, b = -7.5, c = 2.75, d = -2.5

= 5*(-2.5) – (-7.5)*(2.75)

= -12.5 + 20.625

= 8.125 → (2)

Note: The inverse of a matrix is

$$\begin{bmatrix} a & b \\ c & d \end{bmatrix}^{-1} = \frac{1}{Determinant} \cdot \begin{bmatrix} d & -b \\ -c & a \end{bmatrix}$$

So, using (1) and (2) we get,

$$= \frac{1}{8.125} \cdot \begin{bmatrix} -2.5 & 7.5 \\ -2.75 & 5 \end{bmatrix}.$$

58. What is the sum of the positive integral solutions of $|2x - 6| \le 12$?

A. When we remove the modulus sign, we get two possibilities:

Possibility 1:

$$2x - 6 \le 12$$
$$x \le 9 \rightarrow (1)$$

Possibility 2:

$$2x - 6 \geq -12$$

$$x \geq -3 \rightarrow (2)$$

Based on (1) and (2) we get,

-3 ≤ x ≤ 9

The potential integral solutions for x are:

-3, -2, -1, 0, 1, 2, 3, 4, 5,6 ,7, 8, 9

The potential positive integral solutions for x are:

1, 2, 3, 4, 5, 6, 7, 8, 9

Adding these solutions, we get,

= 45.

59. If the radius of a circle is doubled, then what is the percentage change in its area?

A.   Area of circle A is $\pi r^2 \rightarrow$ (1)

If the radius is doubled, the area of circle is,

$$= \pi(2r)^2$$

$$= 4\pi r^2 \rightarrow (2)$$

The percentage change in area is

$$= \frac{(4\pi r^2 - \pi r^2)}{\pi r^2} * 100$$

= 300% increase.

60. How many positive numbers less than 75 are relatively prime to 75?

A.   The prime numbers that divide 75 are:

3⌊75

5⌊25

5⌊5

   1

Thus. the two unique prime numbers that divide 75 are 3, and 5.

The number of multiples of 3 that divide 75 are $75/3 = 25$

→ (1)

The number of multiples of 5 that divide 75 are $75/5 = 15$

→ (2)

The number of multiples of 3*5 that divide 75 are $75/15$

$= 5$ → (3)

Using (1), (2), and (3) the positive numbers less than 75 that are relatively prime to 75 are,

$= 75 - (25 + 15 - 5)$

$= 40$.

61. What is the perimeter of a trapezoid?

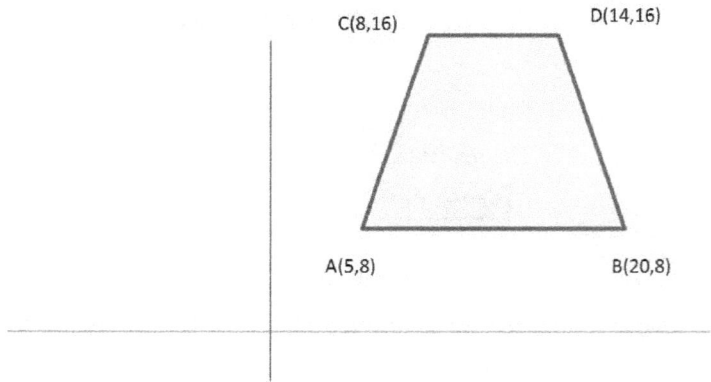

C(8,16)   D(14,16)

A(5,8)   B(20,8)

A. *Note: The distance between two points is calculated as*

$$\sqrt{(y_1 - y_2)^2 + (x_1 - x_2)^2}$$

$\text{len(AB)} = \sqrt{(8 - 8)^2 + (5 - 20)^2} = 15$

$\text{len(AC)} = \sqrt{(8 - 16)^2 + (5 - 8)^2} = \sqrt{73}$

$\text{len(CD)} = \sqrt{(16 - 16)^2 + (8 - 14)^2} = 6$

len(BD) = $\sqrt{(8-16)^2 + (20-14)^2}$ = 10

This, perimeter is sum of all sides =

$15 + \sqrt{73} + 6 + 10$

$= 31 + \sqrt{73}$.

62. Find the distance of point (-2, -5) from its reflection across the line y=3?

A. *The reflection of a point (x, y) in the line parallel to the x-axis (y = a₁) is (x, -y + 2a₁).*

We want the reflection of point (-2, -5) across the line y=3.

Here, x = -2, y = -5 and a_1 = 3.

Thus, the reflection of (-2, -5) in y=3 is, (-2, -5+2*3) = (-2, 1)

The distance between two points is calculated as

$$\sqrt{(y_1 - y_2)^2 + (x_1 - x_2)^2}$$

The distance between (-2, -5) and its reflection (-2, 1) is

$$\sqrt{(-5-1)^2 + (-2-(-2))^2}$$

= 6.

63. If the numbers (5a - 10) and (5b – 25) add up to 145. Find the sum of the numbers ($\frac{a}{3}$ + 5) and ($\frac{b}{3}$ - 7)?

A. Give, 5a - 10 and 5b -25 add up to 145.

5a - 10 + 5b – 25 = 145

5a + 5b - 35 = 145

5(a + b) = 180

a + b = 36 → (1)

Now, let's find sum of ($\frac{a}{3}$ + 5) and ($\frac{b}{3}$ - 7)

($\frac{a}{3}$ + 5) + ($\frac{b}{3}$ - 7)

$= (\frac{a+b}{3} - 2) \rightarrow (2)$

Substituting (1) in (2)

$(\frac{36}{3} - 2)$

$= 10.$

64. If $\frac{5}{3}x = \sqrt{x^2 + 4}$, What is $2x - 12$, if $x>0$?

A. $\frac{5}{3}x = \sqrt{x^2 + 4}$

Squaring both sides.

$(\frac{5}{3}x)^2 = (\sqrt{x^2 + 4})^2$

$\frac{25}{9}x^2 = x^2 + 4$

$25x^2 = 9x^2 + 36$

$16x^2 - 36 = 0$

$(4x + 6)(4x - 6) = 0$

$x = -\frac{3}{2}$ or $x = \frac{3}{2}$

Since x>0, $x = \frac{3}{2}$

So, $2x - 12$

$= 2*\frac{3}{2} - 12$

$= -9.$

65. In a right angled triangle ABC, find AC, if $l(AB) = 12$ and $m\angle A = 32^0$?

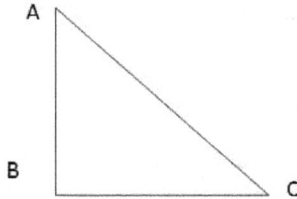

A. We know that,

$$\cos\angle A = \frac{adjacent}{hypotenuse}$$

$$\cos\angle A = \frac{l(AB)}{l(AC)}$$

$$\cos32 = \frac{12}{l(AC)}$$

$$l(AC) = \frac{12}{cos32}$$

$$= 14.15 \text{ units.}$$

66. 11 meter/sec = _____ miles/hour

A. *Note: 1 mile = 1609.34 meters*

Using dimensional analysis, we can write in the below format:

11 meter	1 mile	3600 sec
1 sec	1609.34 meters	1 hour

$$= \frac{3600*11}{1609.34}$$

$$= 24.6 \text{ miles per hour.}$$

67. $\left(\frac{x^{-6}z}{y^{-2}x}\right)\left(\frac{x^2y^3}{x^{-4}y^{-2}z^2}\right)\left(\frac{x^{-3}y^{-4}}{z^4}\right)(xy^{-1}z^3)$

A. *Note: the sign of the power of a variable or a number changes when the variable or number moves from numerator to denominator or vice versa.*

e.g. $\frac{1}{a^n} = a^{-n}$ OR

$$a^n = \frac{1}{a^{-n}}$$

In the problem above, let us move everything from denominator to the numerator to make it easy to perform arithmetic operations, so we have:

41

$$\left(\frac{x^{-6}z}{y^{-2}x}\right)\left(\frac{x^2y^3}{x^{-4}y^{-2}z^2}\right)\left(\frac{x^{-3}y^{-4}}{z^4}\right)(xy^{-1}z^3)$$

$$= (x^{-6}zy^2x^{-1})\,(x^2y^3x^4y^2z^{-2})\,(x^{-3}y^{-4}z^{-4})\,(xy^{-1}z^3)$$

Grouping the x and y terms together to make it easier to simplify, we get,

$$= (x^{-6}x^{-1}\,x^2x^4x^{-3}x)\,(y^2y^3y^2y^{-4}\,y^{-1})(zz^{-2}z^{-4}z^3)$$

$$= (x^{-6-1+2+4-3+1})\,(y^{2+3+2-4-1})(z^{1-2-4+3})$$

$$= (x^{-3}y^2z^{-2})$$

$$= \frac{y^2}{x^3z^2}.$$

68. What is the difference between 12th triangular number and 10th triangular number?

A. *Formula: Triangular number* $a_n = \frac{n(n+1)}{2}$

Thus, the 12th triangular number is,

$$a_n = \frac{n(n+1)}{2} \text{ with } n=12$$

$$a_{12} = \frac{12(12+1)}{2}$$

$$= 78$$

Thus, the 10th triangular number is,

$$a_{10} = \frac{10(10+1)}{2}$$

$$= 55$$

So, the difference between the 12th and 10th triangular numbers is,

78 - 55

$$= 23.$$

69. 3.5 rods = _____ inches?

A. *Formula: 1 rod = 16.5 feet*

and 1 foot = 12 inches

Thus, 3.5 rods = 3.5*16.5 = 57.75 feet

57.75 feet is 57.75*12

= 693 inches.

70. Which inequality matches the graph below:

A. The graph starts at -3 at the lower end (indicated by the circle) and the arrow at the other end indicates that the graph encompasses all the values greater than -3 to +∞. Thus, the inequality is,

$x \geq$ -3.

71. Which of the following is not a function?

(a) $x = -3$ (b) $y = -1$ (c) $y = 2x + 4$ (d) $x^2 - 2y = 12$ (e) $x^4 = y$

A. *Note: A function (y = f(x)) is a relationship where for each value of x, there is one value of y.*

In the above options (c), (d), and (e) as we substitute values for x, we get one resulting value of y.

Option (b) is an independent function, as it is not dependent on x.

Thus, option (a) is the only one where is no relationship between x and y, so it is not a function.

So, the answer is $x = -3$

The other way to look at it is, x = -3 is a line parallel to y axis, so for one value of x, you have infinite values of y.

Thus. it is not a function

72. Can you find which graph below is not a function?

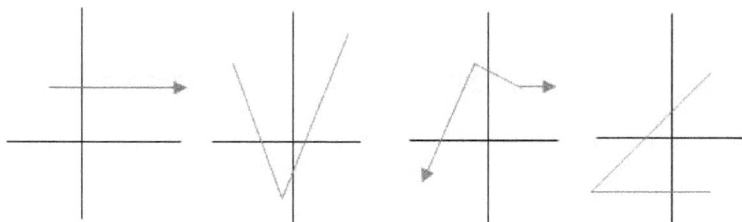

A: *Note: A function (y= f(x)) is where for each value of x, there is only one value for y.*

The first three graphs pass the above test of having one value of y for each value of x.

For the fourth graph, if you apply **the vertical line test for function**, you will notice that for each value of x, there are at times more than one values for y. As shown below by the dotted lines below:

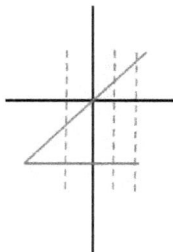

Thus, the fourth graph is not a function.

73. Which of the following represents a direct variation:
(I) $2y = 0.5x + 1$ (II) $4x = 7y$ (III) $5x - 8y = 0$ (IV) $2y = -16$
(a) I only (b) II and III (c) I and III (d) II and IV (e) II only

A. *Note: Direct variation is where one variable changes in proportion to another variable in the form of y = kx, where k is a constant.*

In the above options,

Option I cannot be rearranged to be in the form of $y = kx$.

Option II can be rearranged to be, $y = 0.5x$, which is in the form of $y = kx$.

Option III can be rearranged to be $y = \frac{1}{7}x$, which is in the form of $y = kx$.

Option IV, does not show dependency between the two variables y and x.

Thus, the answers are, option II and III, which is (b).

74. $2\pi =$ _____ minutes

A. *Note: $\pi = 180°$*

Thus, $2\pi = 2 * 180 = 360°$

Also, $1° = 60'$ (minutes)

So, $360° = 360 * 60$

$= 21,600$ minutes.

75. In terms of π, what is the difference between the surface area and the lateral surface area of the cylinder below?

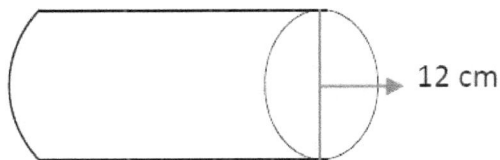

18 cm

A. Here, $r = 12/2 = 6$ cm and

h = 18 cm.

Lateral surface area of the cylinder = $2\pi rh$

Surface area of the cylinder $= 2\pi rh + 2\pi r^2$

The difference between the surface area and the lateral surface area is,

$= (2\pi rh + 2\pi r^2) - 2\pi rh$

$= 2\pi r^2$

$= 2\pi *(6)^2 = 72\pi$ sq cm.

76. If you use matrices to solve

-4x +12 = -4y

2y – 4x = 9

What would be the coefficient matrix?

A. Bring the equations to the standard form of ax + by = c.

So, we have,

-4x + 12 = -4y

-4x + 4y = -12 → (1)

2y - 4x = 9

-4x + 2y = 9 → (2)

We get the coefficient matrix using the x and y coefficients from (1) and (2).

$$= \begin{bmatrix} -4 & 4 \\ -4 & 2 \end{bmatrix}.$$

77. What is the growth rate for the exponential function y = 8(3.7)^x?

A. *Note: the exponential growth function is represented by:* $y = a (1 + r)^t$, *where a is the initial amount, r is the growth rate and t is the time period.*

Here we have,

a = 8 and

1 + r = 3.7, where r is the growth rate.

Solving for r, we get,

r = 2.7

Growth rate is in percentage, so we have

Growth rate = 2.7 * 100

= 270%.

78. Find the volume of an octahedron with side length of $\sqrt{27}$ units?

A: *Note: Volume of an octahedron* $= \dfrac{s^3 \sqrt{2}}{3}$ *where s is the side.*

Here we have s = $\sqrt{27}$.

So, volume = $((\sqrt{27})^3\sqrt{2})/3$

$= \dfrac{(\sqrt{27})^3 \sqrt{2}}{3}$

$= \dfrac{(27\sqrt{27}\sqrt{2}}{3}$

$= \dfrac{(27*3\sqrt{3}\sqrt{2}}{3}$

$= 27\sqrt{6}$ cu. units.

79. Write the solution set in an interval notation for the compound inequality $7 < 3x - 8 \le 28$?

A. *Note: in the interval notation, $\le$ and $\ge$ are represented by "[" and "]" closed brackets and < and > are represented by "(" and ")" open brackets.*

Here we have,

$7 < 3x - 8 \le 28$

$7 + 8 < 3x - 8 + 8 \le 28 + 8$

$15 < 3x \le 36$ (now divide by 3)

$5 < x \le 12$

Thus, in interval notation we will represent this by (5, 12].

80. What is the area of the circle with equation $(x + 4)^2 + (y - 7)^2 = 1600$, where $\pi=3$?

A. *Note: The equation of a circle in standard form is $(x - h)^2 + (y - k)^2 = r^2$.*

Here (h, k) are the coordinates of the center and r is the radius of the circle.

This is also called as the center-radius form of equation of circle.

Here we have $(x + 4)^2 + (y - 7)^2 = 1600$.

Comparing with the standard form, we have the coordinates of the center of the circle as (-4, 7) while, the radius is,

$r^2 = 1600$

$r = 40$

Area of a circle is πr^2

$= \pi (40)^2$

$= 1600\pi$

$= 1600 *3$

$= 4800$ sq units.

81. ABCD is a rectangle inscribed within a circle with center O. If $l(AC) = 4$ cm, then find the area of the circle in terms of π?

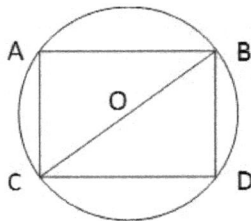

A: Segment BC passing through the origin bisects the right angle ABD.

Thus. $\angle ABC = 45°$.

$$\sin(\text{ABC}) = \frac{opposite}{hypotenuse}$$

$$\sin 45 = \frac{l(AC)}{l(BC)}$$

$$\frac{1}{\sqrt{2}} = \frac{4}{l(BC)}$$

$$l(BC) = 4\sqrt{2}$$

We know that BC is a diameter, so radius is $2\sqrt{2}$

Thus, area of the circle is,

$$= \pi(2\sqrt{2})^2$$

$$= 8\pi \text{ sq. cm.}$$

82. How many lines of symmetry can be drawn in a regular nonagon?

A: *Note: the number of lines of symmetry in a n-sided regular polygon = n.*

A nonagon is an 9-sided regular polygon.

Thus, the number of lines of symmetry for a regular nonagon is 9.

83. Find the proper subsets for the set {1,5,6,9,12,13,18, 20}?

A. *Note: the number of proper subsets in a set with n elements is $2^n - 1$.*

Here, there are 8 elements in the set, so the number of subsets are:

$$= 2^8 - 1$$

$$= 255.$$

84. What is the rate of decay in the exponential decay function y = 1.3(0.45)^x?

A: *Note: the exponential decay function is represented by:*

$y = a (1 - r)^t$, where a is the initial amount, r is the decay rate and t is the time period.

Here we have,

a = 1.3 and

1 - r = 0.45, where r is the decay rate,

Solving for r, we get,

r = 0.55

Decay rate is in percentage, so we have

Decay rate = 0.55 * 100

= 55%.

85. What is the inverse of the matrix:

$$\begin{bmatrix} -3 & 5 \\ 2 & -6 \end{bmatrix}$$

A: *Note: The inverse of matrix* $\begin{bmatrix} a & b \\ c & d \end{bmatrix}$ *is:*

$$\frac{1}{determinant} \begin{bmatrix} d & -b \\ -c & a \end{bmatrix}$$

where, determinant is |ad − bc|

Here, a = -3, b = 5, c = 2, d = -6 → (1)

det = |(-3)(-6) − (5)(2)|

= |18 − 10|

= 8 → (2)

Thus, inverse of $\begin{bmatrix} -3 & 5 \\ 2 & -6 \end{bmatrix}$ is

$$\frac{1}{determinant} \begin{bmatrix} d & -b \\ -c & a \end{bmatrix}$$

Using (1) and (2) we have,

$= \frac{1}{8} \begin{bmatrix} -6 & -5 \\ -2 & -3 \end{bmatrix}$ - multiplying every element inside the matrix with 1/8

$= \begin{bmatrix} -0.75 & -0.625 \\ -0.25 & -0.375 \end{bmatrix}.$

86. What are the coordinates for the vertex of the quadratic
    equation $y = 6x^2 - 10x - 12$

A: *Note: For a quadratic equation $y = ax^2 + bx + c$,*

    the x-coordinate of the vertex $= -\dfrac{b}{2a}$

    and by substituting the value of x in the quadratic

    equation, we calculate the y-coordinate of the vertex.

    Comparing $6x^2 - 10x - 12$ to $ax^2 + bx + c$, we have

    $a = 6$ and $b = -10$

    Since $x = -\dfrac{b}{2a}$

    Thus, $x = -\dfrac{(-10)}{2*6} = 0.8333.... = 0.8\overline{3}$

    Substituting value of x in the equation, we get

    $y = 6(0.8\overline{3})^2 - 10(0.8\overline{3}) - 12$

    $= -16.1666.... = -16.1\overline{6}$

    Thus, the coordinates of the vertex is $(0.8\overline{3}, -16.1\overline{6})$.

87. What is the length of an inner diagonal of a rectangular
    prism that has length of 15 inches, width of 14 inches and
    height of 21 inches?

A.

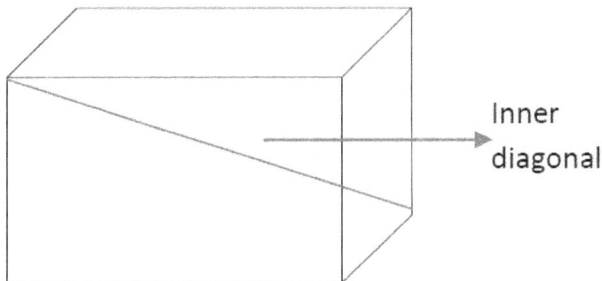

Inner
diagonal

51

Note: The length of inner diagonal of a rectangular prism

is, $\sqrt{length^2 + width^2 + height^2}$.

Here we have length = 15, width = 14 and height = 21,

Thus, the length of the inner diagonal =

$\sqrt{15^2 + 14^2 + 21^2}$

$= \sqrt{862}$ inches.

87. Solution A is a 62% acid solution and solution B is a 26% acid solution. How many liters of solution A must be mixed with solution B to create 48 liters of a 45% acid solution?

A.   Let us say we need to mix "a" liters of solution A with "b" liters of solution B to get to 48 liters of 45% acid solution, so we get:

0.62a + 0.26b = 48 * 0.45

0.62a + 0.26b = 21.6 → (1)

We also know that the total solution is 48 liters, so we have,

a + b = 48 → (2)

Let us solve equations (1) and (2) for the values of a and b.

Multiplying both sides of equation (2) by 0.62,

0.62a + 0.62b = 29.76 → (3)

Subtracting equation (1) through equation (3),

0.36b = 8.16

b = 22.7 liters

Substituting b in equation (2), we get,

a = 25.3 liters.

88.   When divided by x - 2, the polynomial $P(x) = x^5 + 2x^3$ $+Ax + B$, where A and B are constants, the remainder is

equal to 54. When P(x) is divided by x - 4, the remainder is equal 1172. Find A and B?

A. Since we are dividing by x – 2, we can substitute x = 2 in the polynomial equation to get,

$P(2) = 2^5 + 2(2)^3 + A(2) + B$

$= 32 + 16 + 2A + B$

$= 2A + B + 48 \rightarrow (1)$

Given the remainder of (1) is 54, so using remainder theorem, we have

$2A + B + 48 = 54$

$2A + B = 6 \rightarrow (2)$

Also, since we are dividing by x - 4, we can substitute x = 4 in the polynomial equation to get,

$P(4) = (4)^5 + 2(4)^3 + A(4) + B$

$= 1024 + 128 + 4A + B$

$= 4A + B + 1152 \rightarrow (3)$

Given the remainder of (3) is 1172, so using remainder theorem, we have

$4A + B + 1152 = 1172$

$4A + B = 20 \rightarrow (4)$

Subtracting (2) from (4) we get,

$2A = 14$

$A = 7$

Substituting A = 7 in (2), we get B = -8.

89. 2.5 quires are equal to how many gross?

A. *Note: 1 quire = 2 dozen*

and 1 gross = a dozen dozens

Thus, 2.5 quires = 2.5*2 = 5 dozen.

$$= \frac{5}{12}$$

$= 0.42$ gross.

90. What is the range of the graph of the quadratic equation

$f(x) = -7x^2 - x + 8$?

A. *Note: To find the range of a quadratic equation, $ax^2 + bx + c$:*

Step 1 – find the vertex of the quadratic equation $= -\frac{b}{2a}$

Step 2 – If "a" in $ax^2 + bx +$

c is negative, then the function points downwards and the range is $\leq$ the vertex

If the "a" in $ax^2 + bx +$

c is positive, then the function points upwards and the range is $\geq$ the vertex

Here, we have $-7x^2 - x + 8$

where a = -7, b= -1 and c = 8

Let's first calculate the vertex,

$$= -\frac{b}{2a}$$

$$= -\frac{(-1)}{2*(-7)}$$

$$= -\frac{1}{14}$$

$= -0.07$

The next step is to examine the value of "a" to see if it is positive or negative.

Here, a = -7

This means that the quadratic function points downwards and includes the vertex.

Thus, the range of the quadratic function is, y $\leq$ -0.07.

91. What is the sixth heptagonal number?

A. Note: The nth heptagonal number is defined by $\dfrac{n(5n-3)}{2}$

where $n \geq 1$

Here $n = 6$.

So, the sixth heptagonal number is,

$= \dfrac{6(5*6-3)}{2}$

$= 81$.

92. What are the number of regions in a plane determined by 12 lines where no two lines are parallel and only three are concurrent?

A. *Note: The number of regions in a plane of n lines where no two lines are parallel and only three are concurrent is given by the nth triangular number* $= \dfrac{n(n+1)}{2}$.

Here we have 12 lines, so the 12th triangular number would be,

$= \dfrac{12(12+1)}{2}$

$= 78$

Thus, we have 78 regions in a plane determined by 12 lines where no two lines are parallel and only three of these lines are concurrent.

93. $15i^{-4} * 2i^5 * 4i^6 * -4i^3 * i^6 * 6i^{17} * i$

A. *Note: when n is even,*

$i^n = -1$ *when* $n = 2,6,10,...$

$i^n = 1$ *when* $n = 0,4,8,...$

when n is odd,

$i^n = i$ *when* $n = 1,5,9,...$

$i^n = -i$ *when* $n = 3,7,11,...$

Here we have, $15i^{-4} * 2i^5 * 4i^6 * -4i^3 * i^6 * 6i^{17} * i$

Using the above conversions for powers of i we have,

$= 15\frac{1}{i^4} * 2(i) * 4(-1) * -4(-i) * (-1) * 6(i) * i$

$= (15*1) * 2i * (-4) * 4i * -1 * 6i * i$

$= 2880 * i^4$

$= 2880.$

94. $77{,}836 - 21{,}325 =$ _____ Find the remainder and subtract the 10s digit of the remainder from the 1000s digit of the remainder and round off that remainder to ten.

A.   7 7 8 3 6

    - 2 1 3 2 5

    _____

    5 6 5 1 1

The result of the subtraction is 56,511.

Here the 1000s digit is 6 and the 10s digit is 1.

So, the difference of those two numbers is,

$= 6 - 1$

$= 5$

Rounding off this remainder 5 to ten, the answer is 10.

95. In a bag of balls 1/4 are red, 1/6 are blue, 1/10 are yellow and the rest 58 are green. How many balls are red?

A.   Given, 1/4 are red, 1/6 are blue, 1/10 are yellow, so the total balls with those three colors are,

$\frac{1}{4} + \frac{1}{6} + \frac{1}{10} = \frac{31}{60}$

Thus, the remaining balls are

$1 - \frac{31}{60} = \frac{29}{60}$

Given that the remaining balls are green and the count is 58.

If x is the total number of balls, then we have,

$$\frac{29}{60}x = 58$$

x = 120 balls

Thus, the total balls we have are 120.

Given that 1/4th of these balls are red, so we have,

$$\frac{1}{4} * 120$$

= 30 red balls.

96. 2.14 * 2.3 = _____ (nearest hundredth)

A.   2. 1 4

     * 2.3

     _____

     4 2 8 0

    +   6 4 2

     _____

     4. 9 2 2

To round of 4.922 to the nearest hundredth, let's look at the hundredth's term – it is 2, since it is less than 5, we round down

So, the result rounded off the nearest hundredth is 4.92.

97. $25\frac{2}{7} \div 7\frac{1}{7}$

A. $25\frac{2}{7} = \frac{177}{7}$

    $7\frac{1}{7} = \frac{50}{7}$

    Thus, $25\frac{2}{7} \div 7\frac{1}{7}$

    $= \frac{177}{7} \div \frac{50}{7}$

    $= \frac{177}{7} * \frac{7}{50} = \frac{177}{50}$

$= 3\frac{27}{50}.$

98. One dozen apples cost \$4.56, what is the total cost of 3.5 dozen apples, if there is a discount of 10% on total price?

A. Given 1 dozen apples cost \$4.56.

So, the cost of 3.5 dozen apples is

$= 4.56 * 3.5$

$= \$15.96$

At 10% discount, the total price is,

$= 90\%$ of \$15.96

$= 0.9 * 15.96$

$= \$14.36.$

99. The supplement of $\angle m$ is equal to?

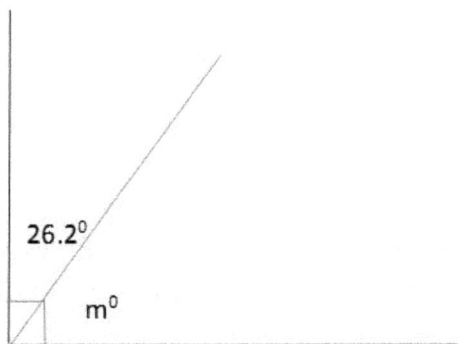

A. *Note: An angle and its supplement add up to 180°*

Here we have, the supplement of m^0

$= 90 + 26.2$

$= 116.2^0$

100. 2,540 cubic inches = _____ gallons

A. 1 cubic inch = 0.004329 U.S. liquid gallons.

Thus, 2,540 cubic inches is,

58

= 2540 * 0.004329

= ~ 11 gallons.

101. If grass grows in your yard each day at twice the rate of previous day and it takes 50 days for your yard to be covered with grass, find out how long it takes for half of your yard to be covered with grass?

A.   The grass covers the yard at twice the previous day and the yard is covered in 50 days, so you can conclude that the yard was half covered with grass on (50 − 1) = 49 days.

102. $\sqrt{3711}$ is between which two integers?

A.   Square of 60 is 3600

And square of 61 is 3721.

So, the $\sqrt{3711}$ is between 60 and 61.

103. If the roman numeral MMCDXLIII were changed into an Arabic number, what would be the sum of its digits?

A.   *Note:*

M=1000

D=500

C=100

L=50

X=10

V=5

I=1

Arabic number is just our regular number system

Operation rules – If the value of a letter is less than the one that follows it, subtract the smaller value from the greater value. This only works when the greater value is within ten times of the smaller value e.g. I & X; C &D.

MM	CD	XL	III
1000+1000	500-100	50-10	1+1+1

= 2000+400+40+3

= 2443

Adding, the digits we get,

= 2 + 4 + 4 + 3

= 13.

104. What is 21.5% of 1100?

A. 21.5% of 1100 is,

= 0.215 * 1100

= 236.5.

105. Change the positive difference of 12,000,000 and 100,000,000 into scientific notation

A. $12,000,000 = 1.2*10^7$

and $100,000,000 = 10*10^7$

$10*10^7 - 1.2*10^7$

$= 8.8*10^7$.

106. A rectangular box is 10 feet high, 11 feet long and 15 feet wide. If the box is filled $1/8^{th}$ with sand, how much of the box does not have sand?

A. *Note: volume of a rectangular box = length * width * height.*

Here, length = 11, width = 15, height = 10.

Thus, the volume of this rectangular box = 11 * 15 * 10 = 1650 cu. feet.

Since $1/8^{th}$ of the box is full of sand, $7/8^{th}$ of the volume is empty

$= \frac{7}{8} * 1650$

$= 1443.75$ cu. feet is empty.

107. What are the odds of drawing out a card with a face from a deck of cards?

A. *Note: Odds are the possibility of an event occurring versus the possibility of the event not occurring.*

There are 4 suits in a standard deck of cards and within each suit there are three types of cards that have faces (King, Queen and Jack).

So, there are 12 cards with faces.

Thus, the possibility of choosing a face card is $\frac{12}{52} =$

$\frac{3}{13}$ $--\to (1)$

And, the possibility of not choosing a face card is $\frac{40}{52} = \frac{10}{13}$

$\to (2)$

Thus, the odds of choosing a face card

$= \dfrac{possibility\ of\ event\ happening}{possiblity\ of\ event\ not\ happening} =$

Divide (1) by (2)

$= \dfrac{\frac{3}{13}}{\frac{10}{13}}$

$= \dfrac{3}{10}.$

108. Find the next term in the sequence -12, -10, -8, -30. -48, -86, -164,…

A. This is an interesting sequence.

If you add the first three terms, you get the fourth term i.e.

-12 -10 -8 = -30

Likewise, if you add the second, third and fourth term,

you get the fifth term i.e. -10 -8 -30 = -48.

And so on…

So, the term following -164, would be the addition of

-164 and the two terms before it in the sequence.

= -48 -86 -164

= -298.

109. If 4x-2y = 10; find $\frac{16^x}{4^y}$?

A. $\frac{16^x}{4^y}$

$= \frac{(2^4)^x}{(2^2)^y}$

$= \frac{2^{4x}}{2^{2y}}$

$= 2^{4x-2y}$ → (1)

Given that $4x - 2y = 10$, so substituting this in (1) we get,

$= 2^{10}$

$= 1024.$

110. One pizza that is sliced can feed one-baker's dozen

people. How many people can eat 10 pizzas?

A. *Note: 1 baker's dozen = 13.*

Given - one pizza can feed one-baker's dozen people, i.e.

13 people.

Thus, 10 pizzas will feed,

= 10 * 13

= 130 people.

111. A rectangle has length that is 3 less than thrice its width

and the perimeter of the rectangle is 42 cm. If the

dimensions of the rectangle are to be dilated by a scale factor of 5, what is the area of the enlarged rectangle?

A. *Let l be the length of the rectangle and w be the width.*

Given, length is 3 less than thrice the width, so we have,

$l = 3w - 3$ → (1)

Perimeter of a rectangle = $2 (l + w)$ → (2)

Substituting (1) in (2) we get,

Perimeter = $2((3w - 3) + w)$

Perimeter = $8w - 6$ → (3)

Given that perimeter is 42 cm, so substituting in (3) we get,

$8w - 6 = 42$

$w = 6$ cm

Substituting in (1), we get

$l = 15$ cm

If the rectangle's dimensions are dilated 5 times, we have

$l = 75$ cm

$w = 30$ cm

Thus, the new area of the dilated rectangle would be,

$= 75 * 30 = 2250$ sq. cm.

112. If L is the lower limit for outliers and U is the upper limit for outliers. What is the value of L and U for the set of data {15, 16, 24, 25, 31, 38, 39, 41, 42, 45, 53}?

A. Step 1: Find the Interquartile Range (IQR):

Let us place parentheses around the numbers above and below the median (which is 38) — it makes Q1 and Q3 easier to find.

(15, 16, 24, 25, 31), (39, 41, 42, 45, 53)

Find Q1 and Q3.

Q1 can be thought of as a median in the lower half of the data. Q3 can be thought of as a median for the upper half of data.

(15, 16, 24, 25, 31), (39, 41, 42, 45, 53)

Q1 = 24 and Q3 = 42.

IQR = Q3 – Q1

= 42 – 24 = 18

IQR = 18

Step 2: Calculate 1.5 * IQR:

1.5 * IQR = 1.5 * 18 = 27

Step 3: Subtract from Q1 to get your lower boundary:

24 – 27 = -3

Step 4: Add to Q3 to get your upper boundary:

42 + 27 = 69.

113. The sum of three consecutive even integers is 306. What is the difference between the first and third integers?

A. Method 1:

Let the three consecutive even integers be 2n, 2n + 2, and 2n + 4.

Given that the sum of these three integers is 306, so we have:

2n + 2n +2 + 2n + 4 = 306

6n + 6 = 306

n = 50

Thus, the three numbers are,

2n = 2 * 50 = 100

2n + 2 = 2* 50 + 2 = 102, and

2n + 4 = 2* 50 + 4 = 104.

The difference between the 1st and 3rd integer is,

$104 - 100 = 4$.

Method 2:

The difference between consecutive even numbers is always 2, so the difference between the first and third consecutive number has to be 4.

114. Simplify $\sqrt{8} + \sqrt[5]{243} + 100^0$

A. $= \sqrt{8} + \sqrt[5]{243} + 100^0$

$= 2\sqrt{2} + (3^5)^{1/5} + 1$

$= 2\sqrt{2} + 3 + 1$

$= 2\sqrt{2} + 4$

$= 2\sqrt{2}\,(1 + \sqrt{2})$.

115. {12,14, 16, 18} U {11, 12, 13, 14, 15} U {11, 13, 15, 17} has how many proper subsets?

A. *Note: the union of two sets are all the elements from each of the two sets.*

If A = {a, b, c, d} and B = {a, c, f, h} then,

AUB = {a, b, c, d, f, h}

Here we have,

{12,14, 16, 18} U {11, 12, 13, 14, 15} U {11, 13, 15, 17}

= {11, 12, 13, 14, 15, 16, 17, 18}

Note: the number of proper subsets in a set with n elements is $2^n - 1$.

Here there are 8 elements in the resulting set, so the proper subsets would be,

$= 2^8 - 1$

$= 255$.

116. In a sock with 8 yellow marbles and 12 black marbles and you make two draws, what is the probability of getting a

black marble and then a yellow marble after replacing the black marble (in ratio form)

A.   There are a total of 8+12 = 20 marbles

The probability of getting a black marble out of 20 marbles is,

$$= \frac{12}{20} = \frac{3}{5} \rightarrow (1)$$

The probability of getting a yellow marble with replacement (makes it total of 20 marbles again) is,

$$= \frac{8}{20} = \frac{2}{5} \rightarrow (2)$$

Thus, the probability of getting a black marble and then with replacement getting a yellow marble is,

(1) * (2)

$$= \frac{3}{5} * \frac{2}{5}$$

$$= \frac{6}{25}.$$

117. What is the sum of all positive integral divisors of the number 120 (inclusive)?

A.   The positive integral divisors of 120 are 1, 2, 3, 4, 5, 6, 8, 10, 12, 15, 20, 24, 30, 40, 60, 120.

The sum of these divisors is,

$= 1 + 2 + 3 + 4 + 5 + 6 + 8 + 10 + 12 + 15 + 20 + 24 + 30 + 40 + 60 + 120$

$= 360.$

118. What is the value of the discriminant of the quadratic equation $\frac{3}{7}x^2 - 5x + 14$?

A.   *Note: For quadratic equation $ax^2 + bx + c = 0$*
the discriminant is $b^2 - 4ac$

Given equation $\frac{3}{7}x^2 - 5x + 14$,

here, $a = \frac{3}{7}$, $b = -5$, $c = 14$

Discriminant is $b^2 - 4ac$

$= (-5)^2 - 4\left(\frac{3}{7}\right)(14)$

$= 1$.

119. What is the linear equation $2y = -\frac{3}{4}x + 12$ written in the standard form?

A. *Note: the standard form of a linear equation is, $ax + by = c$.*

Here we have, $2y = -\frac{3}{4}x + 12$

$8y = -3x + 48$

$3x + 8y = 48$.

120. Using the two right angles below, what is $3x - 2y$?

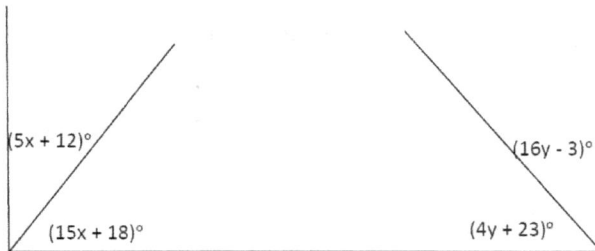

(5x + 12)°

(15x + 18)°

(16y - 3)°

(4y + 23)°

A. Since there are two right angles here, we have

$(15x + 18) + (5x + 12) = 90$

$x = 3 \rightarrow (1)$

$(4y + 23) + (16y - 3) = 90$

$y = 3.5 \rightarrow (2)$

So, using (1) and (2), we have $3x - 2y$ is

$= 3*3 - 2*3.5$

$= 2.$

121. John had $1500 into a bank account compounding at 3% every 6 months. At the end of second year, he gives Andrew half of the interest he accumulated for the 2 years over the principle. How much money will Andrew get?

A. The interest is earned every 6 months, so two years is a period of four 6 months

The balance at the end of the four periods is calculated as,

$P(1 + \frac{r}{100})^t$, where P is the principle, r is the rate of interest and t is the period.

Here we have, P = 1500, r = 3, and t = 4

So, the balance in John's account at the end of 2 years is,

$= 1500(1+ \frac{3}{100})^4$

$= \$1688.26$

Thus, John earned the interest of $1688.26 - $1500 = $188.26 over his principle.

If he gave half of that interest to Andrew, then Andrew received

$= \frac{1}{2} * 188.26,$

$= \$94.13.$

122. If $f(x) = -\frac{1}{9}x^3 - 9$ and $g(x) = \frac{1}{4}x^2 + 12$, find the value of $\frac{-7f(-3)-g(2)}{5}$?

A. We have $f(x) = -\frac{1}{9}x^3 - 9$

So, $f(-3) = -\frac{1}{9}(-3)^3 - 9 = -6 \rightarrow (1)$

We have, $g(x) = \frac{1}{4}x^2 + 12$

So, $g(2) = \frac{1}{4}(2)^2 + 12 = 13 \to (2)$

Thus, to calculate $\frac{-7f(-3)-g(2)}{5}$

Substituting (1) and (2)

$= \frac{(-7)(-6)-13}{5}$

$= \frac{29}{5}$.

123. What is the measure of $\angle w$?

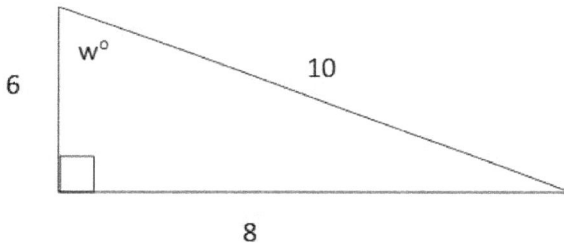

A. $\cos\theta = \frac{adjacent}{hypotenuse}$

Thus, we have here,

$\cos w = \frac{6}{10}$

$w = \cos^{-1}\left(\frac{3}{5}\right)$.

124. What is the volume of a hemisphere with radius of 6 meters in terms of π?

A. *Note: Volume of a hemisphere* $= \frac{2}{3}\pi r^3$.

Here r = 6 meters.

Thus, volume of the hemisphere is,

$= \frac{2}{3}\pi * (6)^3$

$= 144\pi$ cubic meters.

125. Find n, $(\sqrt[3]{7})^{-12})^3 = 7^n$

A. $(\sqrt[3]{7})^{-12})^3$

$= (((7)^{\frac{1}{3}})^{-12})^3$

$= ((7)^{-4})^3$

$= 7^{-12}$

So, we have

$7^n = 7^{-12}$

$n = -12$.

126. Twenty people are in a room and must shake hands with everyone else exactly once. How many handshakes will occur?

A.   With 20 people in the room, the first person will shake hands with 19 people, second person will shake hands with 18 people and so on....

So, the total handshakes will be,

$= 19 + 18 + ... + 1$

Note – the sum of the n consecutive numbers where the first number is a_1 and last number is a_n is

$= \dfrac{n(a_1 + a_n)}{2}$

Here, $a_1 = 1$, $a_n = 19$ and n = 19.

So, we have

$= \dfrac{19(1 + 19)}{2}$ = 190.

127. If $a + 2b = 4$, the area of a square with a side of $4a^2 + 16ab + 16b^2$ is equal to _____ unit^2?

A.   The side of the square is $4a^2 + 16ab + 16b^2$

$= 4(a^2 + 4ab + 4b^2)$

$= 4(a + 2b)^2$ → (1)

Given, $a + 2b = 4$

Substituting in (1), we get

$= 4(4)^2$

$= 64$

So, we get the side of the square to be 64 units.

Thus, area of the square is

$= (64)^2$

$= 4096$ unit^2.

128. Define the exponential decay function that has a decay rate of 4.4%

A. *Note: the exponential decay function is represented by:*

   $y = a (1 - r)^t$, where a is the initial amount, r is the decay rate and t is the time period.

   Here r = 4.4% = 0.044.

   So, the decay function is

   $y = a (1 - 0.044)^t$

   $y = a (0.956)^t$

   where a is a constant and t is the period.

129. If D = the absolute mean deviation of the data set 40, 57, 122, 87 and 157. Find the value of -3D – 6?

A. To find the mean of the data set 40, 57, 87, 122 and 157, let us arrange this data set in ascending order. We get,

   40, 57, 87, 122, 157

   The mean of the above data set is 87.

   Deviation of above data set from the mean is the absolute value of the difference between each value in the data set and the mean.

   $= |40 – 87|, |57 – 87|, |87 – 87|, |122 – 87|, |157 – 87|$

   $= 47, 30, 0, 35, 70$

   The mean absolute deviation of the above data set is the average of the above numbers.

$$= \frac{(47+30+0+35+70)}{5}$$

$= 36.4$

So, -3D - 6 is

$= -3 * 36.4 - 6$

$= -115.2.$

130. Find the area of a polygon with its vertices (-5 -2), (-3, -1), (8, 2), (-4, -7), (2, 1), (0, 5), (1, 3) and (2, 0)?

A. Let us line the points one below another:

A	-5 -2	$(-5)(-1) - (-2)(-3) = -1$
B	-3 -1	$(-3)(2) - (-1)(8) = 2$
C	8 2	$(8)(-7) - (2)(-4) = -48$
D	-4 -7	$(-4)(1) - (-7)(2) = 10$
E	2 1	$(2)(5) - (1)(0) = 10$
F	0 5	$(0)(3) - (5)(1) = -5$
G	1 3	$(1)(0) - (3)(2) = -6$
H	2 0	$(2)(-2) - (0)(-5) = -4$
A	-5 -2	

$$\text{Area} = \left| \frac{-1+2-48+10+10-5-6-4}{2} \right|$$

$= |-21|$

$= 21 \text{ unit}^2.$

131. $0.6\overline{12} = $ _____ (fraction)

A. $0.6\overline{12} = 0.6121212 ....$

$$= \frac{202}{330}$$

132. C is the midpoint of $\overline{AB}$. If the coordinates of A are (16, 10) and the coordinates of C are (-6, -5), then what is the distance of $\overline{AB}$?

A.   If C is the midpoint of $\overline{AB}$, and if $A(x_1, y_1)$ and $B(x_2, y_2)$ and $C(x, y)$, then we have:

$x = \dfrac{x_1 + x_2}{2}$ and

$y = \dfrac{y_1 + y_2}{2}$

Here we have C $(x. y) = (-6, -5)$, A is $(16, 10)$

Let us assume $B(x_2, y_2)$.

So, we have,

$x = \dfrac{x_1 + x_2}{2}$

$-6 = \dfrac{16 + x_2}{2}$

$x_2 = -28$

$y = \dfrac{y_1 + y_2}{2}$

$-5 = \dfrac{10 + y_2}{2}$

$y_2 = -20$

B is $(-28, -20)$

Thus, distance $\overline{AB} = \sqrt{(x_1 - x_2)^2 + (y_1 - y_2)^2}$

$= \sqrt{(16 - (-28))^2 + (10 - (-20))^2}$

$= \sqrt{2836}$

$= 2\sqrt{709}$ units.

133. How many zeroes are at the end of 20!?

A. $20! =$
      $20*19*18*17*16*15*14*13*12*11*10*9*8*7*6*5*4*3*2*1$

There will be four zeroes: two from (20*15), one for 10 and another one for (2*5).

134. What is the sum of all positive integral solutions of the following equation:

$|4x -2| \leq 14$

A. Given, $|4x -2| \leq 14$

$-14 \leq 4x -2 \leq 14$

$-12 \leq 4x \leq 16$

$-3 \leq x \leq 4$

Since we are looking at positive integral solutions only, they are 1, 2, 3, and 4.

Thus, sum of all integral solutions is,

$1 + 2 + 3 + 4$

$= 10.$

135. If the point (-2, -6) is reflected over the line y = x and then rotated 270° counterclockwise about the origin, what are its new coordinates?

A. Reflection of point (x, y) reflected on x-axis is (y, x).

The reflection of a point (-2, -6) over the line y = x, is (-6, -2).

Rotation of point (x, y) 270° counterclockwise about the origin is (y, -x), so here the transformation of point (-6, -2) is (-2, 6).

136. Simplify $(\sqrt{2} + 1)^3 - 4\sqrt{8}$

A. $(a + b)^3 = a^3 + 3a^2b + 3ab^2 + b^3$

Thus, $\left(\sqrt{2} + 1\right)^3$

$= (\sqrt{2})^3 + 3(\sqrt{2})^2(1) + 3\sqrt{2}(1)^2 + (1)^3$

$= 2\sqrt{2} + 6 + 3\sqrt{2} + 1$

$= 5\sqrt{2} + 7 \rightarrow (1)$

We have, $\left(\sqrt{2} + 1\right)^{3} - 4\sqrt{8}$

Substituting (1) in the above equation we get,

$= 5\sqrt{2} + 7 - 4\sqrt{8}$

$= 5\sqrt{2} + 7 - 8\sqrt{2}$

$= -3\sqrt{2} + 7.$

137. Complete the square to solve the quadratic equation

$3x^2 + 6x + \underline{\hspace{1cm}} = 6 + \underline{\hspace{1cm}}$ by completing the square, what would you add to both sides of the equal sign?

A. $3(x^2 + 2x + \underline{\hspace{0.5cm}}) = 6 + \underline{\hspace{0.5cm}} \rightarrow (1)$

The left side of the equation is in the format of $ax^2 + bx + c$. Thus, the square can be completed by adding $(b/2)^2$

Here we have b = 2.

So, to complete the square we add

$(2/2)^2$

= 1 to the left side in the parenthesis $\rightarrow$ (2)

Substituting (2) on the left side in (1) we get,

$3(x^2 + 2x + 1)$

This now means we would need to add 3 to the right hand side of the equation in (1) as well, in order to still keep the equation balanced.

$3(x^2 + 2x + 1) = 6 - 3$

$3(x^2 + 2x + 1) = 9$

$(x^2 + 2x + 1) = 3$

$(x + 1)^2 = (\sqrt{3})^2$

Thus, as you can see, we had to add 3 to both sides to get to a perfect square.

138. What is the unit's digit of 21^8?

A. $21^8 = 21^2 * 21^2 * 21^2 * 21^2$

$= 441 * 441 * 441 * 441$

So, the unit's digit will be $1 * 1 * 1 * 1 = 1$

OR looking at it the other way, when we have a number that has 1 in the units place and we raise this number to any power, the units digit of the result is always 1.

139. If arc AC = 35° and arc AD = 130°, what is the measure of $\angle ABC$?

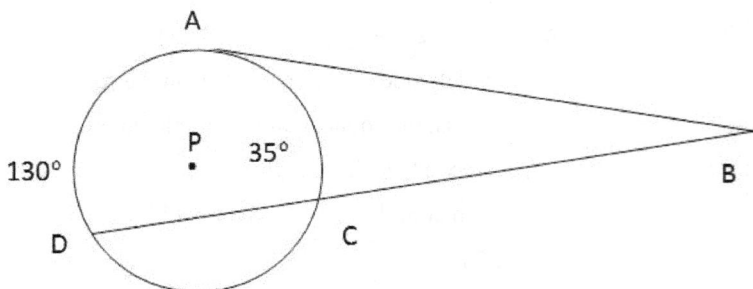

A. $\angle ABC = \frac{1}{2}(m(\overset{\frown}{AD}) - m(\overset{\frown}{AC}))$

$= \frac{1}{2}(130 - 35)$

$= 47.5°$.

140. Simplify $\frac{-2}{3-\sqrt{7}}$?

A. $\frac{-2}{3-\sqrt{7}}$

Rationalizing denominator by multiplying numerator and denominator by $3 + \sqrt{7}$.

$\frac{-2}{3-\sqrt{7}} * \frac{3+\sqrt{7}}{3+\sqrt{7}}$

$$= \frac{-2(3+\sqrt{7})}{(3)^2 - (\sqrt{7})^2}$$

$$= \frac{-2\,(3+\sqrt{7})}{2}$$

$$= -(3 + \sqrt{7}).$$

141. John has 40 coins that are quarters and dimes. The total of coins is $8.50. If John finds 10 additional dimes, what will be the value of all the dimes that John has?

A. Let us assume that John has q quarters and d dimes.

Given,

$q + d = 40$ → (1)

Given,

$0.25q + 0.1d = 8.5$ → (2)

Multiplying (1) by 0.1 and subtracting it from (2) we get

$0.25q - 0.1q + 0.1d - 0.1d = 8.5 - 4$

$0.15q = 4.5$

$q = 30$

Substituting in (1), $d = 10$.

If John finds 10 more dimes, then he will have $10 + 10 = 20$ dimes

And the total value of all those dimes will be $0.1 * 20 = \$2$.

142. After simplifying, what is the denominator of the following?

$$\frac{2x^5 - 8x^3 - x^2 + 4}{x^3 - 2x^2 - x + 2} \div \frac{3x^2 + 6x - 9}{x^2 - 1} \cdot \frac{6(x-1)}{2x^2 + 4x + 2}$$

A. $$\frac{2x^5 - 8x^3 - x^2 + 4}{2x^3 - 4x^2 - x + 2} \div \frac{3x^2 + 6x - 9}{x^2 - 1} \cdot \frac{6(x-1)}{2x^2 + 4x + 2}$$

$$= \frac{2x^3(x^2 - 4) - (x^2 - 4)}{x^2(x-2) - (x-2)} \cdot \frac{x^2 - 1}{3x^2 + 6x - 9} \cdot \frac{6(x-1)}{2(x^2 + 2x + 1)}$$

$$= \frac{2x^3(x^2-4)-(x^2-4)}{x^2(x-2)-(x-2)} \cdot \frac{(x+1)(x-1)}{3(x^2+2x-3))} \cdot \frac{6(x-1)}{2(x+1)(x+1)}$$

$$= \frac{(2x^3-1)(x^2-4)}{(x^2-1)(x-2)} \cdot \frac{(x+1)(x-1)}{3(x^2+3x-x-3)} \cdot \frac{6(x-1)}{2(x+1)(x+1)}$$

$$= \frac{(2x^3-1)(x+2)(x-2)}{(x+1)(x-1)(x-2)} \cdot \frac{(x+1)(x-1)}{3(x(x+3)-(x+3))} \cdot \frac{6(x-1)}{2(x+1)(x+1)}$$

$$= \frac{(2x^3-1)(x+2)(x-2)}{(x+1)(x-1)(x-2)} \cdot \frac{(x+1)(x-1)}{3(x-1)(x+3)} \cdot \frac{6(x-1)}{2(x+1)(x+1)}$$

$$= \frac{(2x^3-1)(x+2)}{(x+3)(x+1)(x+1)}$$

Thus, the denominator is $(x + 3)(x + 1)(x + 1)$.

143. $132_5 + 31_6 + 50_7 = 225_8 - \underline{}_9$

A. $\underline{132}_5 = \underline{1}*5^2 + \underline{3}*5^1 + \underline{2}*5^0 = 42$ → (1)

$\underline{31}_6 = \underline{3}*6^1 + \underline{1}*6^0 = 19$ → (2)

$\underline{50}_7 = \underline{5}*7^1 + \underline{0}*7^0 = 35$ → (3)

Thus, $121_5 + 34_6 + 52_7$ – adding (1), (2) and (3)

$= 42 + 19 + 35$

$= 96$ → (4)

Also, we have,

$\underline{225}_8 = \underline{2}*8^2 + \underline{2}*8^1 + \underline{5}*8^0 = 149$ → (5)

Thus, substituting (4) and (5) we get,

$132_5 + 31_6 + 50_7 = 225_8 - \underline{}_9$, we get,

$96 = 149 - \underline{}_9$

$\underline{}_9 = 53$

To convert 53 to base 9:

Step 1:

$$
\begin{array}{r}
(\; 5 \;) \\
9 \; \overline{\smash{\big)}\; 53} \\
-45 \\
\hline
(\; 8 \;)
\end{array}
$$

Make a note of the remainder 8 → (6)

Step 2:

Divide the quotient from Step 1 by 9

$$
\begin{array}{r}
9 \; \overline{\smash{\big)}\; 5} \\
\hline
(\; 5 \;)
\end{array}
$$

Since we cannot divide 5 any further by 9, the remainder of Step 2 is 5.

We get 53 to base 9 by collating the remainders from step 1 and 2, except in the reverse order. The remainder from Step 1 is 8 and remainder of Step 2 is 5, so collating them in reverse order we get, 58

Thus 53 converted to base 9 is 58.

144. What is the sum of the first 35 even numbers?

A.   The first 35 even numbers are: 2, 4, 6, 8, ….

The nth number in a series can be calculated as

$a_n = a_1 + (n - 1)d$

where a_1 is the first number in the series and d is the difference between two consecutive numbers in the series.

Here, we have n = 35 and d = 2

$a_{35} = a_1 + (n-1)d$

$= 2 + (35-1)2$

$a_{35} = 70$

The sum of n numbers in a series can be calculated as,

$$= \frac{n(a_1 + a_n)}{2}$$

The sum of 35 numbers in the series is,

$$= \frac{35(2+70)}{2}$$

$= 1,260.$

145. $1999 + 9999 + 102 = ?$

A.   Breaking this down to,

$1999 + 9999 + 100 + 1 + 1$

$= (1999+1) + (9999 + 1) + 100$

$= 12100.$

146. What is the probability of rolling a pair of dice and getting a sum less than 5?

A.   The total combinations when you roll a pair of dice are,

$= 6 * 6 = 36$

The combinations that result in sum of less than 5 are (1, 1), (1, 2), (2, 2), (1, 3), (2, 1), (3, 1) = 6 combinations

Thus, the probability is,

$$= \frac{6}{36}$$

$$= \frac{1}{6}.$$

147. $12\frac{2}{7} \div 2\frac{1}{7}$

A. $12\frac{2}{7} = \frac{86}{7}$

$2\frac{1}{7} = \frac{15}{7}$

$12\frac{2}{7} \div 2\frac{1}{7}$

$$= \frac{86}{7} \div \frac{15}{7}$$

$$= \frac{86}{7} * \frac{7}{15}$$

$$= \frac{86}{15}.$$

148. What is the sum of the 4th triangular number and the largest palindrome less than 570?

A. *Formula: nth Triangular number* $a_n = \frac{n(n+1)}{2}$

Palindrome is a word or number that reads the same backward and forward.

Let us find the 4th triangular number, so n = 4,

$$a_4 = \frac{4(4+1)}{2}$$

$= 10 \rightarrow (1)$

The largest palindrome number that reads the same forward and backward and is less than 570 is 565 $\rightarrow$ (2)

So, the sum of (1) and (2) is,

$= 10 + 565$

$= 575.$

149. 2.5 pints = _____ ounces?

A. *Note: 1 pint = 16 fluid ounces*

Thus, 2.5 pints is

$= 2.5 * 16$

$= 40$ ounces.

150. Let A = number of vertices of a dodecagonal prism. Let B = number of edges of a rectangular prism. Find the value of A^2 – B^2?

A. *Note: The number of vertices of a dodecagonal prism are 24.*

The number of edges of a rectangular prism are 12.

Thus, A = 24 and B = 12.

So, $A^2 - B^2$ is,

$= 24^2 - 12^2$

$= 432.$

151. If $y = -\frac{2}{3}x - 1$ and the y coordinate of the point on the line $6n^6$, what is the x coordinate?

A. Given $y = -\frac{2}{3}x - 1 \rightarrow (1)$

and the y coordinate is $6n^6$

Substituting we get,

$6n^6 = -\frac{2}{3}x - 1$

$x = -(\frac{18n^6+3}{2}).$

152. $\sqrt{324i^4}$ - 1

A. We know that $\sqrt{324} = 18$ and $i^2 = -1$

So, $\sqrt{324i^4}$ - 1

$= 18i^2 - 1$

$= 18(-1) - 1$

$= -19.$

153. What are three or more lines that meet at a certain point? What is the point of intersection called?

A. When three or more lines intersect at a point, they are concurrent lines and the point of intersection is called the point of concurrency.

154. What is the average of all distinct prime factors of 363?

A. The distinct prime factors of 363 are 3 and 11.

The average of these prime factors is (3+11)/2 = 7.

155. If f(x) = x - 4, g(x) = x^3 and h(x) = 5 – x^2, find the value of f(-4) + g(-2) + h(8)?

A. $f(x) = x - 4$

So, f(-4)

$= -4 - 4 = -8 \rightarrow (1)$

$g(x) = x^3$

So, g(-2)

$= (-2)^3$

$= -8 \rightarrow (2)$

$h(x) = 5 - x^2$

So, h(8)

$= 5 - 8^2$

$= -59 \rightarrow (3)$

So, by substituting (1), (2) and (3), we get

$f(-4) + g(-2) + h(8)$

$= -8 - 8 - 59$

$= -75.$

156. 10 gallon = ___ pints?

A.   *Note: 1 quart = 0.25 gallon*

10 gallons is,

$= 10/0.25 = 40$ quarts $\rightarrow (1)$

Note: 1 quart = 2 pints

40 quarts are,

$= 40 * 2 = 80$ pints.

157. Calculate the difference of 150,000,000,000,000 –

18,000,000,000,000 into scientific notation?

A. $150,000,000,000,000 = 1.5 * 10^{14}$

$18,000,000,000,000 = 0.18 * 10^{14}$

Thus, $150,000,000,000,000 - 18,000,000,000,000$

$= 1.5 * 10^{14} - 0.18 * 10^{14}$

$= 1.32 * 10^{14}.$

158. What is the difference between the complement and supplement of 42.5^0?

A. The complement of $42.5^0 = 90 - 42.5$

$= 47.5^0$

The supplement of $42.5^0 = 180 - 42.5$

$= 137.5^0$

Thus, the difference between the complement and supplement of 42.5^0 is,

$= 137.5 - 47.5$

$= 90^0$.

159. Calculate $x^2 - 2x + 1$, if 4x is to 20 as 12 is to 192.

A. Given that 4x is to 20 as 12 is to 192

$$\frac{4x}{20} = \frac{12}{192}$$

$$x = \frac{5}{16}$$

Thus, $x^2 - 2x + 1$

$$= (\frac{5}{16})^2 - 2 (\frac{5}{16}) + 1$$

$$= \frac{25 - 160 + 256}{256}$$

$$= \frac{121}{256}.$$

160. A rectangular tank 25 ft by 10 ft by 10 ft. is 75% filled with water, how much water is in the tank?

A. Volume of the tank

$= 25 * 10 * 10$

$= 2500$ cu. ft.

Since it is 75% full of water, the amount of water in the tank is,

$= 0.75 * 2500$

$= 1,875$ cu. ft.

161. If the point (-1, -11) is reflected across the y-axis, what is the sum of the new coordinates of the point?

A.   *Note – the point (x, y) reflected across y-axis is (-x, y) and the point (x, y) reflected across x-axis is (x, -y).*

So, the point (-1, -11) reflected across y-axis is (1, -11).

The sum of the new coordinates of the point are

$= 1 - 11$

$= -10$.

162. $\angle CAD$ is a central angle of 35° and radius of the circle is 12 inches. What is the length of arc CBD? Assume $\pi = 3$.

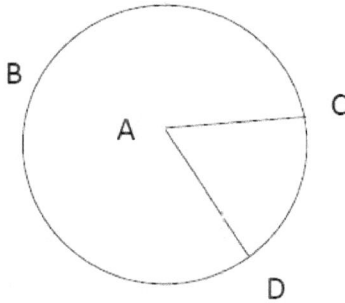

A. $l(\widehat{CD}) = \dfrac{central\ angle}{360} * circumference\ of\ the\ circle$

$l(\widehat{CD}) = \dfrac{35}{360} * 2 * 3 * 12$

$= 7$ inches

Thus, $l(\widehat{CBD}) = circumference\ of\ the\ circle - l(\widehat{CD})$

$= 2 * 3 * 12 - 7 = 65$ inches.

163. Simplify: $\dfrac{4^2 - 4}{8^2 + 6^2}$

A. $\dfrac{4^2 - 4}{8^2 + 6^2}$

$$= \frac{16 - 4}{64 + 36}$$

$$= \frac{3}{25}.$$

164. What are the odds of rolling a pair of dice and getting a sum less than or equal to 7?

A. We know that the outcomes from rolling a pair of dice are 36.

Let us write down the combinations of getting 7 or less:

1. 1, 1
2. 1, 2
3. 1, 3
4. 1, 4
5. 1, 5
6. 1, 6
7. 2, 2
8. 2, 3
9. 2, 4
10. 2, 5
11. 3, 3
12. 3, 4
13. 2, 1
14. 3, 1
15. 4, 1
16. 5, 1
17. 6, 1
18. 3, 2
19. 4, 2
20. 4, 3
21. 5, 2

Thus, the odds of getting 7 or less is $\frac{21}{36}$ or $\frac{7}{12}$ → (1)

So, the odds of not getting 7 or less is $\frac{(36-21)}{36}$ or $\frac{5}{12}$ → (2)

Using (1) and (2), the odds of getting 7 or less are

$$= \frac{7}{12} \div \frac{5}{12}$$

$$= \frac{7}{5}.$$

165. Find the degree of the monomial $(a^{15}b^5c^7)^3$?

A. *Note: the degree of the monomial is the sum of the powers of all its variables.*

Here we have,

$(a^{15}b^5c^7)^3$

$= (a^{45}b^{15}c^{21})$

Thus, the degree of the monomial is the sum of the powers of the variables

$= 45 + 15 + 21$

$= 81$.

166. Find the next term in the sequence: 2, 18, 84, 260,…

A. The series is in the form of $n^4 + n$,

e.g. 1st number in the series is found by substituting $n = 1$

$= 1^3 + 1 = 2$

2nd number in the series is found by substituting $n = 2$

$= 2^4 + 2 = 18$

3rd number in the series is found by substituting $n = 3$

$= 3^4 + 3 = 84$

So, the 5th number of the series is found by substituting n

$= 5$

$= 5^4 + 5 = 630$.

167. How much money would be in a bank account after depositing $15,000 into a simple interest account for 60 months at a rate of 5%?

A. Simple Interest earned every year is Principle * interest rate

= 15000 * 0.05

= $750

So, simple interest earned for 5 years is

= 750 * 5

= $3,750

Thus, the money in the account after 60 months would be the principle and the earned interest

= 15000 + 3750

= $18,750.

168. Use the picture below and find the measure of ∠CEA?

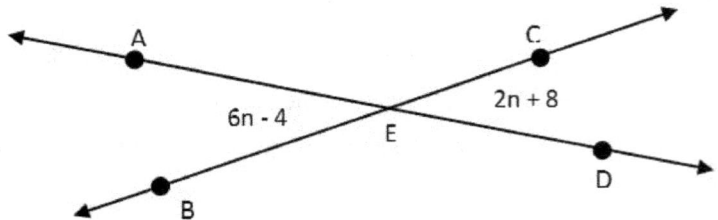

A. We know that when two lines intersect the vertical angles are congruent,

∠AEB = ∠CED

6n - 4 = 2n + 8

n = 3

Thus, ∠CED = 2 * 3 + 8

= 14^0

We know that

$\angle CEA + \angle CED = 180^0$

$\angle CEA + 14 = 180$

$\angle CEA = 166°$.

169. A hexagon's angles are in a ratio of 2:4:6:6:8:10. What is the measure of the largest angle?

A. *Note: the sum of interior angles of a polygon with n sides is 180 (n – 2).*

Here we have a pentagon, so n = 6.

So, the sum of interior angles of a pentagon is

= 180 (6 – 2)

= 720

Given that the angles in a pentagon are in a ratio of 2:4:6:6:8:10.

If x is the multiplicative factor for the ratio of angles, we have,

2x + 4x + 6x + 6x + 8x + 10x = 720

36x = 720

x = 20

The measure of the largest angle is 10x

= 10 * 20

= 200°.

170. If QQQ + θθ = 20 and QQ - θ = 4? What is 3θ?

A. Let us call Q = x and θ = y, so we have

3x + 2y = 20 → (1) and

2x – y = 4 → (2)

(2) * 2

4x – 2y = 8 → (3)

7x = 28

$x = Q = 4$

Substituting in (2) and solving we get

$y = \theta = 4$

Thus, $3\theta = 3 * 4 = 12$.

171. What is type of quadrilateral with no parallel sides?

A. A rectangle, rhombus, trapezoid, rhomboid (shaped like a rhombus) have at least a pair of parallel sides – a trapezium has no parallel sides.

172. Find the next number in the sequence: -4, 8, -29, 17, -54, 26, …

A. If you look at every other number, they together form a pattern:

e.g. -4, -29, -54, ….

If you add -25, to the previous number, you get the next number

Similarly, if you look at:

8, 17, 26, ….

If you add 9, to the previous number, you get the next number.

Thus, the next number in the pattern after -4, 8, -29, 17, -54, 26, …

$= -54 - 25 = -79$.

173: Find the area of the parallelogram?

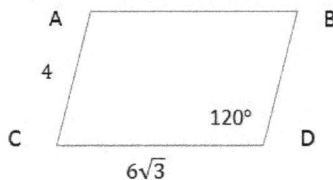

A. Area of parallelogram = base * height

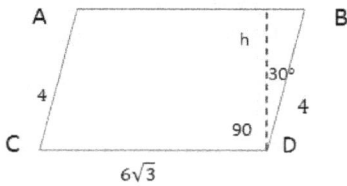

$$\cos 30 = \frac{adjacent}{hypotenuse}$$

$$\frac{\sqrt{3}}{2} = \frac{h}{4}$$

$$h = 2\sqrt{3}$$

So, base = $6\sqrt{3}$ and height = $2\sqrt{3}$

Thus, the area of the parallelogram = base * height.

$$= 6\sqrt{3} * 2\sqrt{3}$$

=36 sq. units.

174. How many vertices does a dodecagonal prism have?

A. A dodecagon has 12 sides.

   A regular dodecagonal prism looks like the following:

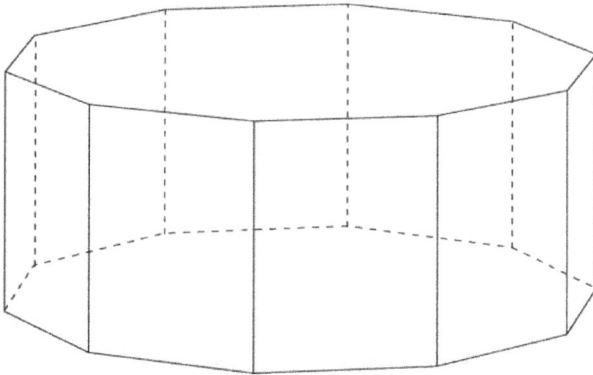

So, as you can see, it has 14 faces, 36 edges and 24 vertices.

175. Given $a - b = 5$ and $a^2 + b^2 = 11$. Find $a^3 - b^3$?

A.   Given $a - b = 5$

Squaring both sides, we get

$(a - b)^2 = 5^2$

$a^2 - 2ab + b^2 = 25$

Rearranging the above we get,

$a^2 + b^2 - 2ab = 25$

We know that $a^2 + b^2 = 11$

$11 - 2ab = 25$

$ab = -7 \rightarrow (1)$

We know that $a^3 - b^3 = (a - b)(a^2 + ab + b^2)$

Substituting $a - b = 5$, $a^2 + b^2 = 11$, and $ab = -7$ we get,

$5 * (11 - 7) = 20$.

176. Solve $-4 + 36 \div (6 . 3) + 28 \div 4$

A.   The order of operations in this case will be first solve the parenthesis and then go from left to right solving for multiplication and division.

So, we have,

$-4 + 36 \div (6 . 3) + 28 \div 4$

$= -4 + 36 \div 18 + 28 \div 4$

$= -4 + \dfrac{36}{18} + \dfrac{28}{4}$

$= -4 + 2 + 7$

$= 5$.

177. A $(-7, 9)$ is located on the coordinate plane. If A is translated 8 units to the right and down 10 units, what is the sum of A's new coordinates?

A.   A$(-7, 9)$

If you move A by 8 units to the right, the new x coordinate of A is

$= -7 + 8 = 1$.

If you move A by 10 units down, then the new y coordinate of A is

$= 9 - 10 = -1$

Thus, the new coordinates of A are $(1, -1)$

The sum of the new coordinates of A is

$= 1 + (-1)$

$= 0$.

178. A bag contains 10 red, 12 blue, 14 green, 8 yellow, and 6 brown balls. What are the odds of drawing a red or yellow ball from the bag?

A. Total balls are $10 + 12 + 14 + 8 + 6 = 50$.

There are 10 red balls, so the odds of drawing a red ball is

$\frac{10}{50} = \frac{1}{5} \rightarrow (1)$

There are 8 yellow balls, so the odds of drawing a yellow

ball is $\frac{8}{50} = \frac{4}{25} \rightarrow (2)$

There are 12 blue balls, 14 green balls and 6 brown balls, so the odds of not drawing a red or yellow balls are,

$= \frac{12+14+6}{50} = \frac{32}{50}$

$= \frac{16}{25} \rightarrow (3)$

Thus, the odds of drawing a red or yellow ball is

$= \frac{odds\ of\ drawing\ a\ red\ ball + odds\ of\ drawing\ a\ yellow\ ball}{odds\ of\ not\ drawing\ a\ red\ or\ yellow\ ball}$

Using (1), (2) and (3) we get

$= \frac{\frac{1}{5} + \frac{4}{25}}{\frac{16}{25}}$

$= \frac{9}{16}$.

179. If a Δ b $= 2a^2 - b^2$, then find the value of $-2 \Delta (5 \Delta -3)$?

A. Given, a Δ b $= 2a^2 - b^2$

We have (5 Δ -3), so here a $= 5$ and b $= -3$

$(5 \Delta -3) = 2*5^2 - (-3)^2$

$= 50 - 9$

$= 41 \rightarrow (1)$

We have to solve for -2 Δ (5 Δ -3)

Substituting (1), we get -2 Δ 41

Here a $= -2$ and b $= 41$

$(-2 \Delta 41) = 2*(-2)^2 - (41)^2$

$= -1673.$

180. What is the harmonic mean 4 and 12?

A. The harmonic mean of two numbers a and b is,

$$= \frac{2}{\frac{1}{a}+\frac{1}{b}}$$

Here the two numbers are 4 and 12, so the harmonic mean is,

$$= \frac{2}{\frac{1}{4}+\frac{1}{12}}$$

$= 6.$

181. If determinant of matrix $\begin{bmatrix} 4 & a \\ -6 & -2 \end{bmatrix}$ is 10, find the value of a?

A. *Note: Determinant of matrix is* $\begin{bmatrix} a & b \\ c & d \end{bmatrix} = ad - bc$

$\begin{bmatrix} 4 & a \\ -6 & -2 \end{bmatrix} = (4)(-2) - (a)(-6) = -8 + 6a \rightarrow (1)$

Given determinant is 10

So, comparing to (1) we get,

$-8 + 6a = 10$

$a = 3.$

182. 100 yards + 2 mile = _____ feet?

A. *Note: 1 yard = 3 feet*

    and 1 mile = 5280 feet

    100 yards + 2 mile

    = 3*100 + 2*5280

    = 10,860 feet.

183. How many faces does a hexagonal pyramid have?

A. A hexagonal pyramid has a base of a hexagon, so to form a pyramid, there will be six faces on top of the base and then there will the hexagonal base itself.

    Thus, the total faces of a pentagonal pyramid will be,

    = 6 + 1

    = 7.

184. What is 7 more than the abscissa of the point (-3, 8)?

A. *Note: Abscissa is the distance of a point from y-axis, so basically it is the x coordinate of a point.*

    Here the point is (-3, 8)

    So, the abscissa (x coordinate) here is -3.

    7 more than the abscissa is,

    = -3 + 7

    = 4.

185. In $\triangle ABC$ below, $\angle B = 60°$ and $\overline{BC} = 12$ units. The   length of $\overline{AD}$ is equal to?

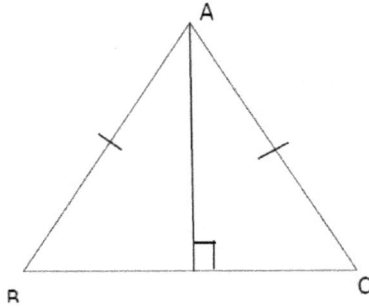

A. Since, $\overline{AB} = \overline{AC}$, $\triangle ABC$ is an isosceles triangle and $\overline{AD}$

bisects $\overline{BC}$

Thus, we have $\overline{BD}$ = 6 units

Using trigonometry, we have,

$$\tan(angle) = \frac{Opposite}{Adjacent}$$

$$\tan\angle B = \frac{\overline{AD}}{\overline{BD}}$$

$$\tan 60 = \frac{\overline{AD}}{\overline{BD}}$$

$$\sqrt{3} = \frac{\overline{AD}}{6}$$

$\overline{AD} = 6\sqrt{3}$ units.

186. Points (5, -5) and (-4, -6) are on a line. If the line is translated down by 3 units, what is the new equation of the line in standard form?

A. The line passes through points (5, -5) and (-4, -6).

The line is translated down 3 units, so the y coordinates would change and x coordinates would stay the same.

The new points would be

(5, -5) → (5, -5-3) = (5, -8) and

(-4, -6) → (-4, -6-3) = (-4, -9)

Thus, the translated new points are (5, -8) and (-4, -9).

To find the new equation of line, let us first find the slope of line n through these new points:

$$\text{Slope} = \frac{y_1 - y_2}{x_1 - x_2}$$

Thus, slope $= \dfrac{-9 - (-8)}{-4 - 5}$

$$\text{Slope} = \frac{1}{9}$$

Thus, the equation of line n is

$$y - y_1 = \text{slope}(x - x_1)$$

$$y - (-8) = \frac{1}{9}(x - 5)$$

$$9y + 72 = x - 5$$

x -9y = 77 is the new equation of line in standard form.

187. What is the largest unattainable sum of the numbers 14 and 10?

A. *Note: the largest unattainable sum of two numbers a and b is*

= ab – (a + b)

Here we have a = 14 and b = 10,

So, the largest unattainable sum of these two numbers is,

= 14 * 10 – (14 + 10)

= 116.

188. How many combinations can be made from 8 colors taken 5 at a time?

A. *Note: the combinations of n things taken r at a time is,*

$$^{n}C_r = \frac{n!}{r!(n-r)!}$$

Here we have n = 8 and r = 5,

$$^{8}C_5 = \frac{8!}{5!(8-5)!}$$

$$= \frac{8*7*6}{3*2*1}$$

$$= 56.$$

189. For an equation $2x^2 - 7x + a = 0$, a is a constant. If 2 is one of the solutions of this equation, what is the value of a?

A. Since 2 is a solution, we can substitute it in the given equation to calculate a:

$2(2)^2 - 7(2) + a = 0$

$8 - 14 + a = 0$

$a = 6.$

190. What is the length of the median of the right trapezoid?

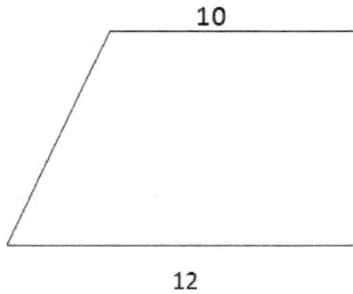

A. The median of a trapezoid is the line joining midpoints of the non-parallel sides

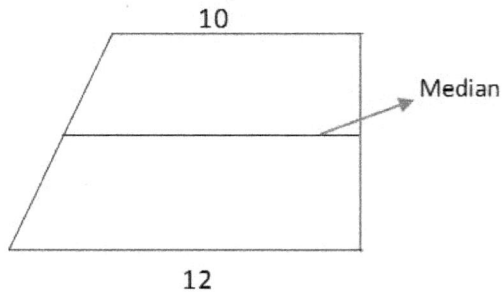

Note: *The length of the median of a trapezoid is the average of the lengths of the two parallel sides (bases).*

$= \frac{1}{2} * (10 + 12)$

$= 11.$

191. If $A = \begin{bmatrix} 1 \\ -2 \end{bmatrix}$ and $B = [-4 \quad -9]$ then A. B $= \begin{bmatrix} a & b \\ c & d \end{bmatrix}$. Find the value of $a + b + c - d$?

A. The product of a matrix that is 2*1 with another matrix that is 1*2, will produce a matrix that is 2*2

Thus, we have,

$\begin{bmatrix} 1 \\ -2 \end{bmatrix} * [-4 \quad -9]$

$= \begin{bmatrix} (1) * (-4) & (1)(-9) \\ (-2)(-4) & (-2)(-9) \end{bmatrix}$

$= \begin{bmatrix} -4 & -9 \\ 8 & 18 \end{bmatrix}$ → (1)

Given A.B $= \begin{bmatrix} a & b \\ c & d \end{bmatrix}$

Comparing with (1), we get

$a = -4, b = -9, c = 8,$ and $d = 18$

Thus, $a + b + c - d$

$= -4 - 9 + 8 - 18$

$= -23.$

192. $(a^{-3}b^3)(3a^2b^5)(a^3)^2(-5a^{-4}b^2)(a^{-2}b^{-3})^0$

A. Anything raised to the power of 0 is 1

Let us simplify the terms raised to powers

$(a^{-3}b^3)(3a^2b^5)(a^3)^2(-5a^{-4}b^2)(1)$

Bringing like terms together we get,

$= (3 * -5)(a^{-3} * a^2 * a^6 * a^{-4}) (b^3 * b^5 * b^2)$

$= -15ab^{10}.$

193. Using the interval notation, what is the solution to the following inequality?

$5x - 8 < 17$

A. *Note: in the interval notation, $\leq$ and $\geq$*

are represented by "[" and "]" closed brackets

While, $<$ and $>$ are represented by "(" and ")" open

brackets

5x – 8 < 17

5x < 25

x < 5

This means x can have all the values from -∞ up to but

not including 5.

In interval notation, this is represented by (-∞, 5).

194. Find the area of a regular dodecagon that has an apothem

of 12 cm and a side length of 20 cm?

A. *Note: the area of a regular polygon that has n sides is,*

$Area = \frac{1}{2} * apothem * perimeter$

Perimeter = n * length of each side

Apothem is a line from the center of a polygon to any of

its sides and forms a right angle with the side

Here we have a regular dodecagon so, the number of sides

n = 12

Also, given that the apothem is 12 cm

Length of the side of the dodecagon is 20 cm

Thus, the perimeter of the dodecagon is

= n * length of the side

= 12 * 20

= 240 cm

Let us now calculate the area of the dodecagon

$Area = \frac{1}{2} * apothem * perimeter$

$Area = \frac{1}{2} * 12 * 240$

= 1,440 sq.cm.

195. Find the vertical asymptote of the rational function y = $\frac{5x-2}{2x-6}$?

A. *Note: Vertical asymptote is a line that a rational function comes close to, but never touches. To find a vertical asymptote, we set the denominator of the function to 0 and solve for x.*

Here we have 2x - 6 in the denominator. So we get,

2x – 6 = 0

x = 3 is the vertical asymptote.

197. What is the domain of the function in the following graph?

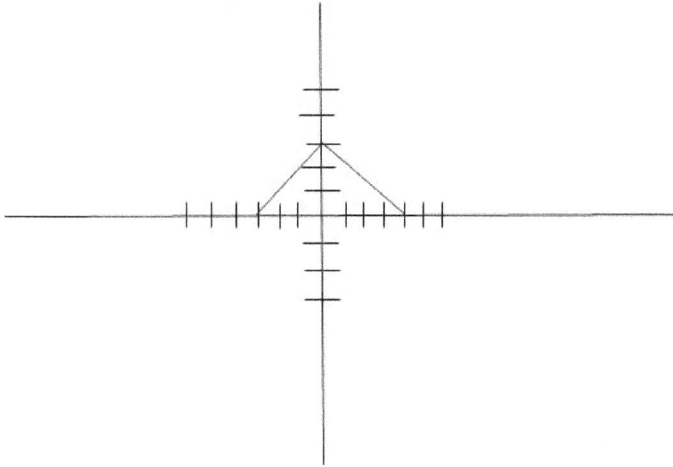

A. The domain of the function are the bounds in which the function is defined.

As you can see from the graph, the bounds for x values are between -3 and +4, so the domain of the function is

$-3 \leq x \leq 4$

While for y it would be,

$-\infty \leq y \leq 3$.

198. Bob has 30% of $150. Pam has 60% of Bob's amount. What percent of $150 does Pam have?

A.   Given, Bob has 30% of $150.

Pam has 60% of Bob's amount, so Pam will have,

= 60% of 30% of $150

= 18% of $150.

199. If $f(x, y, z) = -x^3 - \dfrac{z}{y}$. find f(-2, 3, -6)

A.   Given, $f(x, y, z) = -x^3 - \dfrac{z}{y}$

Let's calculate f(-2, 3, -6)

Here x = -2, y = 3, z = -6

$f(-2, 3, -6) = -(-2)^3 - \dfrac{(-6)}{3}$

= 10.

200. How many zeroes will there be in the product of $2^4 * 5 * 2^4 * 3 * 10^3 * 5$

A.   Let us simplify the numbers,

= 16 * 5 * 16 * 3 * 1000 * 5

Let us rearrange numbers to see if we can avoid doing this long multiplication.

= 16 * 5 * 16 * 5 * 3 * 1000

As you can see 16 * 5 will result in a zero in the unit's place. We have two of them, so we will have two zeros. We also have three zeros from 1000, so the total zeros in the product result will be 5 zeros.

201. If $(100 - 10^5)^2 - (100 + 10^5)^2 = -4 * 10^x$. Find x?

A. Let a = 100 and b = 10^5

So, we have $(a - b)^2 - (a + b)^2$

$= a^2 - 2ab + b^2 - (a^2 + 2ab + b^2)$

$= -4ab$

$= -4*100*10^5$

$= -4*10^7$

Comparing to $-4 * 10^x$ we get,

x = 7.

202. Factor: $4x^4 - 256$

A. $4x^4 - 256$

$= 4(x^4 - 64)$

$= 4(x^2 - 8)(x^2 + 8)$

$= 4(x + 8)(x - 8)(x^2 + 8)$.

203. 10 couples have 4 unique anniversary dates among them. What is the most couples who could share the same anniversary dates?

A. Since there are 4 unique anniversary dates, there will be 4 couples with those unique anniversary dates. There will be $10 - 4 = 6$ couples with same anniversary date as the one of the other 4. Thus, there will be at most $6 + 1 = 7$ couples with the same anniversary dates.

204. Find total degrees in a regular 50-sided polygon?

A. *Note: Sum of interior angles of a regular polygon of n-sides is, (n-2) * 180*

Here we are being asked to find out the sum of all interior angles of a regular polygon of 50 sides.

We have n = 50, so the sum of all interior angles is

$= (50 - 2) * 180$

= 8640.

205. $\triangle\triangle\triangle + \square\square = 18$ and $\triangle + \square = 30$; what is the value of $\square*\triangle$?

A. Let x represent $\triangle$ and let y represent $\square$

Given,

3x + 2y = 18 → (1)

x + y = 30 → (2)

Solving for y, we multiply (2) by 3 to get,

3x + 3y = 90 → (3)

Subtract (1) from (3) we get,

y = 72 or $\square$ = 72

Substituting in (2), we get x = -42 or $\triangle$ = -42

Thus, $\square*\triangle$= 72 * (-42) = -3024.

206. If the equation of a circle is $(x - 2)^2 + (y + 4)^2 = 64$, what is 50% of the circumference of the circle? $\pi = 3$.

A. *Note: the center-radius equation form of circle is:*

$(x - h)^2 + (y - k)^2 = r^2$

where (h, k) are coordinates of the center of the circle and r is the radius of the circle.

Comparing the given equation of the circle $(x - 2)^2 + (y + 4)^2 = 64$, with the center-radius equation form $(x - h)^2 + (y - k)^2 = r^2$, we can calculate radius of the circle,

$r^2 = 64$

r = 8

Thus, 50% of the circumference of the circle = 0.5 * $2\pi r$

= 0.5 * 2 * 3 * 8

= 24.

207. What is the acute angle formed between the hands of the clock at 7 minutes past 4 o' clock?

A. One complete rotation of the minute hand of a clock or a circle represents 360°

1 hour = 60 minutes = 360°

Thus, each minute or the clock represents = $\frac{360}{60} = 6^0$

Since we are looking at 7 minutes past 4 o' clock, the 7 minutes would represent

= 7 * 6 = 42^0 → (1)

Now let us look at the hour's hand –

There are 12 hours on a clock, so each hour represents

= $\frac{360}{12} = 30^0$

Thus, at 4 pm, the hour's hand will be at

= 30 * 4 = 120° → (2)

However, we are looking at 7 minutes past 4, the hour hand won't be exactly at 4, but will be somewhere between 4 and 5.

We can see that 7 minutes represent $\frac{7}{60} = \frac{7}{60}$th of the hour.

So, the additional movement of the hour hand after 7 min past 4 would be,

= $\frac{7}{60}$ * 30 = 3.5° → (3)

Thus, using (2) and (3) after 7 min past 4 the hour's hand will be at

= 120 + 3.5 = 123.5° → (4)

Thus, using (1) and (4), at 7 min past 4, the angle between the hours and min hands would be

= 123.5 – 42

= 81.5°.

208. Find the permutations that can be made from 8 objects taken 3 at a time?

A. *Note: the permutations of n things taken r at a time is,*

$$^nP_r = \frac{n!}{(n-r)!}$$

Here we have n = 8 and r = 3,

$$^{10}P_4 = \frac{8!}{(8-3)!}$$

$$= \frac{8*7*6*5!}{5!}$$

$$= 336.$$

209. Write the inverse to the conditional statement to the contrapositive statement "if not m, then not n?"

A. Given that the contrapositive statement is "if not m, then not n"

Where the first part with "if" is the hypothesis and the second statement is an action or conclusion.

To get to the conditional statement from the contrapositive statement, flip the places of the hypothesis and conclusion/action part of the statements and take out the negatives from both.

So, the conditional statement to the contrapositive statement "if not m, then not n" is,

"if n, then m"

To get the inverse of this conditional statement, convert the hypothesis and the action/conclusion to negatives

"if not n, then not m."

210. $\frac{11}{18}\pi = $ _____ degrees

A. *Note: 1 radian = 180/π degrees*

Thus, $\frac{11}{18}\pi$ radians

$$= \frac{11}{18}\pi * \frac{180}{\pi}$$

$= 110^0$.

211. The average age of 20 students in Class A is 10 years. In Class B, the average age of 30 students is 15. If the classes are combined what would be the average age?

A.   Let the sum of the ages of all students in Class A be M and let the sum of ages of all the students in Class B be N. Given, for Class A with 20 students, the average age is 10, so we have,

$$\frac{M}{20} = 10$$

M = 200 years – this is the sum of all ages in Class A → (1)

Given that for Class B of 30 students, the average age is 15, so we have,

$$\frac{N}{30} = 15$$

N = 450 years – this is the sum of all ages in Class B → (2)

When the classes are combined, the total students in the class will be,

$= 20 + 30 = 50$ students

To calculate the average age of this combined class, we need to add all the ages from Class A and all the ages from Class B and divide that by the total number of students.

$$= \frac{M+N}{50}$$

Using (1) and (2), we know that all the ages in Class A add up to 200 years and Class B add up to 450 years.

$$= \frac{200+450}{50}$$

= 13 years

The average age of the combined class is 13 years.

212. Robert fills up tank in 14 min. Jack fills up tank in 20 min. If it takes Robert, Jack, and James to together fill the tank in 8 min. How long would it take for James to fill the tank?

A. Robert fills up tank in 14 min, so he fills $1/14$th of the tank in 1 min.

Jack fills up tank in 20 min, so he fills $1/20$th of tank in 1 min.

Let James fill the tank in j min, so he fills $1/j$th tank in 1 min.

Together they fill the tank in 8 min, so they fill $1/8$th of tank in 1 min.

So, we have,

$$\frac{1}{14} + \frac{1}{20} + \frac{1}{j} = \frac{1}{8}$$

$$\frac{1}{j} = \frac{1}{8} - \frac{1}{14} - \frac{1}{20}$$

$$\frac{1}{j} = \frac{1}{280}$$

$$j = 280$$

Thus, it will take James 280 min to fill the tank on his own.

213. If two triangles are similar and the sides of one triangle are 4, 13, 20 and the smallest side of the second triangle is 11, what is the longest side of the second triangle?

A. Since the two triangles are similar, we have,

$$\frac{smallest\ side\ of\ first\ triangle}{longest\ side\ of\ first\ triangle} = \frac{smallest\ side\ of\ second\ triangle}{longest\ side\ of\ second\ triangle}$$

So, here we have,

$$\frac{4}{20} = \frac{11}{longest\ side\ of\ second\ triangle}$$

$$longest\ side\ of\ second\ triangle = \frac{11*20}{4}$$

= 55 units.

214. A square S1 has a perimeter of 40 inches and another square S2 has a perimeter of 52 inches. What is the difference between the area of the bigger square and smaller square?

A. *Note: If a is the length of the side of any square, then the perimeter of that square is 4a.*

Given, square S1 has a perimeter of 40 inches.

So, we have,

4a = 40

a = 10 inches.

Thus, the length of side square S1 is 10 inches.

The area of square S1 will be

$= 10^2 = 100$ sq inches

Given, square S2 has a perimeter of 52 inches.

So, we have,

4a = 52

a = 13 inches.

Thus, the length of side square S2 is 13 inches.

The area of square S2 will be

$= 13^2 = 169$ sq inches

Thus, the difference between area of S2 and S1 is

= 169 – 100

= 69 sq inches

215. What is $log_{25}5$?

A. We know that if $log_a b = c$, then $a^c = b$.

Let $log_{25} 5 = m$

Then, $25^m = 5$

$5^{2m} = 5^1$

Comparing, we get

$2m = 1$

$m = \frac{1}{2}$ or square-root.

216. Find the positive difference between the growth factor of the exponential function $y = (\frac{7}{5})^x$ and the decay factor of the exponential decay function $y = \frac{1}{2}. 0.85^x$?

A. *Note: the exponential growth function is represented by:*

   $y = a (1 + r)^x$, where a is the initial amount, r is the growth rate, $(1 + r)$ is the growth factor, and x is the time period.

   And, the exponential decay function is represented by:

   $y = a (1 - r)^x$, where a is the initial amount, r is the decay rate, $(1 - r)$ is the decay factor, and x is the time period.

   Given, the exponential growth function is $(\frac{7}{5})^x$.

   Comparing with the standard exponential growth equation, we see that, the growth factor is,

   $= \frac{7}{5} = 1.4 \rightarrow (1)$

   Given, the exponential decay function is $\frac{1}{2}. 0.85^x$.

   Comparing with the standard exponential decay equation, we see that the decay factor is,

   $= 0.85 \rightarrow (2)$

   Thus, the difference between the two factors is the difference of (1) and (2)

$= 1.4 - 0.85$

$= 0.55$.

217. A cylindrical container has radius of 12m and height of 20m. If the container is half full, what is the volume of the liquid in the container? (use $\pi = 3$)

A. *Note: the volume of a cylinder is $\pi r^2 h$.*

Given, the height of the cylinder, h = 20m and the radius r = 12m.

Thus, using the formula for the volume of the cylinder we have,

$= \pi r^2 h$

$= 3(12)^2 20$

$= 8,640$ cu. m.

The container is only half full, so the volume of the liquid is,

$= \frac{1}{2} * 8640$

$= 4,320$ cu. m.

218. If you have $1 worth of pennies, $0.5 worth of dimes and $0.75 worth of nickels in your pocket. What is the probability that you will randomly be able to get a nickel from your pocket?

A. Since you have $1 worth of pennies, you have 100 pennies → (1)

Since you have $0.5 worth of dimes, you have 5 dimes → (2)

Since you have $0.75 worth of nickels, you have 15 nickels → (3)

So, using (1), (2) and (3), you have total of 100 + 5 + 15 = 120 coins in your pocket.

You have 15 nickels, so randomly finding a nickel out of

15 nickels is $^{15}P_1 = \frac{15!}{(15-1)!} = 15$ → (4)

To select one coin out of a total of 120 coins in your

pocket is, $^{120}P_1 = \frac{120!}{(120-1)!} = 120$ → (5)

So, using (4) and (5), the probability of drawing a nickel

from your pocket is $\frac{15}{120} = \frac{1}{8}$.

219. Find the approximate geometric mean of 8, 5, 2^2, 10, 2?

A. *Note: If there are n numbers, then geometric mean is the*
    nth root of the product of all the n numbers.

    The geometric mean of these 5 numbers is

    $= \sqrt[5]{8 * 5 * 2^2 * 10 * 2}$

    $= \sqrt[5]{8 * 5 * 4 * 10 * 2}$

    $= \sqrt[5]{3200}$

    $= \sim 5$.

220. What is x, if $4\log x + 8\log 2 = \log 16$?

A. *Note: $a\log b = \log b^a$ and*

    $\log a + \log b = \log(ab)$

    $4\log x + 8\log 2 = \log 16$

    $\log x^4 + \log 2^8 = \log 16$

    $\log(2^8 x^4) = \log 16$

    $\log(256x^{4)} = \log 16$

    $256x^4 = 16$

    $x^4 = \frac{1}{16}$

    $x = \frac{1}{2}$.

221. What is the shortest distance from the line with the equation 2x - 4y = -6 and the point (4,0)?

A. The shortest distance from a point to a line is a perpendicular line.

Given that the equation of the line is

2x - 4y = -6, let's simplify

$$y = \frac{x}{2} + \frac{3}{2}$$

The slope of this line is 1/2.

The slope of the line perpendicular to this line is -2.

This perpendicular line passes through (4, 0), so the equation of this line is.

$$y - 0 = -2 (x - 4)$$

$$y = -2x + 8$$

$$y + 2x = 8 \rightarrow (1)$$

Let us assume that this perpendicular line in equation (1) intersects the line 2x - 4y = -6 at points (a, b). So, the point (a, b) will satisfy the equations of both the lines

We will have,

$$2a - 4b = -6 \rightarrow (2) \text{ and}$$

$$b + 2a = 8 \rightarrow (3)$$

Subtract (2) from (3)

$$5b = 14$$

$$b = \frac{14}{5}$$

Substituting in (3) we get,

$$a = \frac{13}{5}$$

Thus, the coordinates of the point where the two lines perpendicularly intersect are $(\frac{13}{5}, \frac{14}{5})$

Let's calculate the distance is the distance between the two points (4, 0) and $(\frac{13}{5}, \frac{14}{5})$

The distance between two points is calculated as

$$\sqrt{(y_1 - y_2)^2 + (x_1 - x_2)^2}$$

$$= \sqrt{(0 - \frac{14}{5})^2 + (4 - \frac{13}{5})^2}$$

$$= \sqrt{(\frac{196}{25} + \frac{49}{25})}$$

$$= \frac{7\sqrt{5}}{5} \text{ units.}$$

222. Simplify $\sqrt{12} + 2\sqrt[4]{48}$

A. $\sqrt{12} + 2\sqrt[4]{48}$

$$= 2\sqrt{3} + 2\sqrt[4]{16 * 3}$$

$$= 2 * 3^{1/2} + 4\sqrt[4]{3}$$

$$= 2 * 3^{1/2} + 4 * 3^{1/4}$$

$$= 2\sqrt[4]{3}(\sqrt[4]{3} + 2).$$

223. Find the area between two concentric circles $(x - 2)^2 + (y - 4)^2 = 36$ and $(x - 2)^2 + (y - 4)^2 = 81$?

A. We know that the equation of a circle is $(x - h)^2 + (y - k)^2 = r^2$, where (h, k) is the center of the circle and r is the radius.

Here we have two concentric circles $(x - 2)^2 + (y - 4)^2 = 36$ and $(x - 2)^2 + (y - 4)^2 = 81$.

So, the radius of inner circle is $r_1^2 = 36$; $r_1 = 6$ units.

And the radius of outer circle is $r_2^2 = 81$; $r_2 = 9$ units.

Thus, the area between the two concentric circles is,

$$= \pi (r_2^2 - r_1^2) = \pi(9^2 - 6^2)$$

$$= 45\pi \text{ sq. units.}$$

224. What is the area of quadrilateral ABCD?

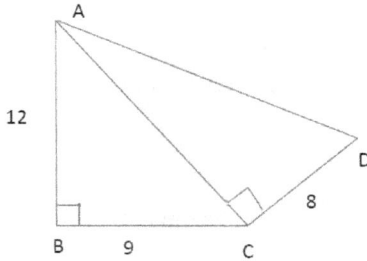

A. As you can see, the quadrilateral ABCD can be broken
    into two right triangles:

    $\triangle ABC$ and $\triangle ACD$

    The area of $\triangle ABC$ is,

    $= \frac{1}{2} * 12 * 9$

    $= 54$ sq units $\rightarrow (1)$

    To find the area of $\triangle ACD$, let us first find out the length
    of height AC of that triangle.

    Applying Pythagoras theorem, we have

    $l(AC)^2 = l(AB)^2 + l(BC)^2$

    $l(AC)^2 = 12^2 + 9^2$

    $l(AC) = 15$ units.

    Thus, the area of $\triangle ACD$ is,

    $= \frac{1}{2} * 15 * 8$

    $= 60$ sq units $\rightarrow (2)$

    Thus, the area of quadrilateral ABCD = sum of the areas
    of $\triangle ABC$ and $\triangle ACD$.

    Adding (1) and (2)

    $= 54 + 60$

    $= 114$ sq units.

225. If f(0) = 3, f(2) = 7, f(5) = 13, and f(9) = 21, find f(16)?

A. We have a series like the following:

3, __ , 7, __ , __ , 13, __ , __ , __ , 21 → (1)

We seem to have a series that is of the form

f(n) = 3 + 2n where n ≥ 0 → (2)

You can validate by substituting n = 0, 2, 5 and 9 and you will get the pattern shown in (1)

To get to the 16th number in the series, let us substitute n = 16 in (2)

f(16) = 3 + 2*16

= 35.

226. Find the coefficient of the term x^7y^6 when $(x + y)^9$ is expanded?

A. *Note: In binomial theorem $(x + y)^n$, the coefficient of a term is given by $^nC_{r-1}$ where r is the order of the term after the expansion. Remember to order them where the order of x is decreased first and order of y is increased later.*

We need to calculate $(x + y)^9$, so n = 9.

The term x^7y^6 will be the 3rd term in the order; so here r = 3.

$= {}^nC_{r-1}$

$= {}^9C_2$

$= \dfrac{9!}{(9-2)!(2!)}$

= 36.

227. The Fibonacci sequence is 0, 1, 1, 2, 3, 5, ...Find the sum of the first 10 terms of the sequence?

A. In a Fibonacci sequence, the next number is found by summing the previous two numbers

Thus, the first 10 numbers in Fibonacci sequence are: 0, 1, 1, 2, 3, 5, 8, 13, 21, 34.

$$= 0 + 1 + 1 + 2 + 3 + 5 + 8 + 13 + 21 + 34$$

$$= 88.$$

228. $\begin{bmatrix} 3 & 3 \\ -2 & -5 \end{bmatrix} \begin{bmatrix} -4 & -5 \\ -1 & -7 \end{bmatrix} = \begin{bmatrix} A & -36 \\ 13 & B \end{bmatrix}$. What is $A^2 - 2AB + B^2$?

A. $\begin{bmatrix} 3 & 3 \\ -2 & -5 \end{bmatrix} \begin{bmatrix} -4 & -5 \\ -1 & -7 \end{bmatrix}$

$$= \begin{bmatrix} 3*(-4) + 3(-1) & 3*(-5) + 3(-7) \\ -2*(-4) + (-5)(-1) & -2*(-5) + (-5)(-7) \end{bmatrix}$$

$$= \begin{bmatrix} -15 & -36 \\ 13 & 45 \end{bmatrix}$$

Comparing to $\begin{bmatrix} A & -36 \\ 13 & B \end{bmatrix}$, we get

A = -15

and B = 45

So, $A^2 - 2AB + B^2 = (-15)^2 - 2(-15)(45) + (45)^2$

$$= 3600.$$

229. C is the midpoint of $\overline{AB}$, E is the midpoint of $\overline{AC}$ and D is the midpoint of $\overline{CB}$. If the length of $\overline{EC} = 2x - 4$ and the length of $\overline{AB} = x + 5$. What is the length of $\overline{EB}$?

A. Let us draw a rough sketch of the above information:

A   E   C   D   B

$$l(\overline{EC}) = l(\overline{AE}) = 2x - 4$$

$$l(\overline{AC}) = l(\overline{AE}) + l(\overline{EC})$$

$$= 2x - 4 + 2x - 4$$

$$= 4x - 8 \rightarrow (1)$$

C is the midpoint of $\overline{AB}$,

Given, $l(\overline{AB}) = x + 5$

Thus, $l(\overline{AC}) = \frac{x+5}{2} \rightarrow (2)$

Comparing (1) and (2) we get,

$4x - 8 = \frac{x+5}{2}$

$8x - 16 = x + 5$

$x = 3$

So, $l(\overline{AE}) = 2x - 4$

$= 2*3 - 4$

$= 2$ units $\rightarrow$ (3)

And, $l(\overline{AB}) = x + 5$

$= 3 + 5$

$= 8$ units $\rightarrow$ (4)

We know that $l(\overline{EB}) = l(\overline{AB}) - l(\overline{AE})$

Substituting (3) and (4) we get

$l(\overline{EB}) = 8 - 2$

$= 6$ units.

230. $\frac{15}{74}$ (base 10) = ___$_6$

A. Let us first convert 15 to base 6.

Step 1: Let us divide 15 by 6 to get the quotient and the remainder.

$$6\lfloor 15$$

$$\lfloor 2 - \text{quotient}$$

We have 3 as the remainder $\rightarrow$ (1)

Step 2: Let us divide the quotient from step 1 which is 2 by 6 to get the quotient and the remainder.

$$6\lfloor 2$$

We have 2 as the remainder (as 2 cannot be divided by 6) $\rightarrow$ (2)

Since we cannot divide this any further, we have everything that we need to convert 15 to base 6, we do this by using remainders from steps (1) and (2), but use them in the reverse order.

So, we take 3 from (1), 2 from (2) and stack them in the reverse order to get 23 → (3)

Let us now convert 74 to base 6.

Step 3: Let us divide 74 by 6 to get the quotient and the remainder.

$$6\lfloor 74$$

$$\lfloor 12 - \text{quotient}$$

We have 2 as the remainder → (4)

Step 4: Let us divide the quotient from step 3 which is 12 by 6 to get the quotient and the remainder

$$6\lfloor 12$$

$$\lfloor 2 - \text{quotient}$$

We have 0 as the remainder → (5)

Step 5: Let us divide the quotient from step 4 which is 2 by 6 to get the quotient and the remainder

$$6\lfloor 2$$

We have 2 as the remainder (as 2 cannot be divided by 6) → (6)

Since we cannot divide this any further, we have everything that we need to convert 74 to base 6, we do this by using remainders from steps (4), (5), and (6), but use them in the reverse order.

So, we take 2 from (4), 0 from (5), and 2 from (6) and stack them in the reverse order by to get 202 → (8)

Thus, using (3) and (8) we get, $\frac{15}{74}$ (base 10)

$= \frac{23}{202}$ (base 6).

231. Solve $-3|7x - 9| \geq -15$

A. $-3|7x - 9| \geq -15$

Dividing by -3 on both sides, the relationship changes from $\geq$ to $\leq$)

$|7x - 9| \leq 5$

So, we have two conditions,

$7x - 9 \leq 5$ and

$7x - 9 \geq -5$

So, if $7x - 9 \leq 5$, then

$7x \leq 14$

$x \leq 2 \rightarrow (1)$

We also have $7x - 9 \geq -5$

$7x \geq 4$

$x \geq 0.571 \rightarrow (2)$

From (1) and (2) we get,

$0.571 \leq x \leq 2.$

232. If a pentagon has vertices (6, 2), (-4, -2), (3. 4), (8, 5), and (-2, 7), what is the area?

A.   Let us line the points one below another:

A   6   2 $6(-2) - 2(-4) = -4$

B   -4   -2

                       $-4(4) - (-2)(3) = -10$

C   3   4

                       $3(5) - 4(8) = -17$

D   8   5

                       $8(7) - 5(-2) = 66$

E   -2   7

                       $(-2)(2) - 7(6) = -46$

A   6   2

$$\text{Area} = \left| \frac{-4-10-17+66-45}{2} \right|$$

= 5.5 sq units.

233. A building 300m tall. If your angle of elevation to the building is 30^0, find the length of the shadow cast by the building?

A. *Note: the angle of elevation is the angle between the horizontal plane and the straight line drawn from the eye of the observer to the top of the object.*

Here we have,

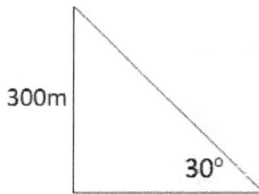

$$\tan\theta = \frac{Opposite}{Adjacent}$$

To find the length of the shadow,

$$\tan 30 = \frac{300}{length\ of\ shadow}$$

$$\frac{1}{\sqrt{3}} = \frac{300}{length\ of\ shadow}$$

Length of shadow = $300\sqrt{3}$ m.

234. For the function represented below, find y where x = -8?

x	-1	3	-3	7	-5
y	-3	-15	3	-27	3

A. Let us represent the relationship between x and y as:

y = ax + b → (1)

Based on the values in the table we have,

$y = -3$ for $x = -1$

Substituting in (1) we get,

$-3 = -a + b$ → (2)

Based on the values in the table we also have,

$y = -15$ for $x = 3$

Substituting in (1) we get,

$-15 = 3a + b$ → (3)

Solving for and b, let us subtract (3) from (2)

$12 = -4a$

$a = -3$

Substituting value of a in (2) we get,

$-3 = 3 + b$

$b = -6$

Substituting in (1) we get

$y = -3x - 6$ → (4)

This is a linear function, so to find y for $x = -8$, we substitute in (4).

$y = -3*(-8) - 6$

$y = 18.$

235. How many ounces are 3 pecks?

A. *Note: 1 US peck = 297.89 US fluid ounces*

3 pecks = 3 * 297.89

= 893.67 ounces.

236. How many faces does a dodecahedron have?

A. Each face of a platonic solid is a similar regular polygon. A dodecahedron has 12 faces.

237. A boat is going with the current to the shore 6 miles away takes 1.5 hours, but it takes it 3 hours to come back while

going against the current. What is the speed of the current?

A. Let the speed of the boat be b mph and the speed of the current be c mph.

When the boat goes with the current, we have:

Distance = speed * time

Distance = 6 miles, time = 1.5 hrs and since the boat is going with the current, the actual speed is (b + c), so we have,

6 = (b + c) * 1.5

6 = 1.5b + 1.5c → (1)

When the boat goes against the current, we have:

Distance = 6 miles, time = 3 hrs and since the boat is going against the current, the actual speed is (b - c), so we have.

6 = (b - c) * 3

6 = 3b – 3c → (2)

To calculate b, let us do (1) * 2 and add to (2), so we get

18 = 6b

b = 3 mph

Substituting in (1), we get,

6 = 1.5*3 + 1.5c

c = 1 mph

So, the speed of the current is 1 mph.

238. $(44 + 26)^2 – (13 – 3)^2$

A. $(44 + 26)^2 – (13 – 3)^2$

$= (70)^2 – (10)^2$

As you notice, this is in the form of $a^2 – b^2$

$= (a + b)(a – b)$

Here we have a = 70 and b = 10, thus

$(70)^2 - (10)^2$

$= (70 + 10)(70 - 10)$

$= 80 * 60$

$= 4800.$

239. Find the perimeter of the figure?

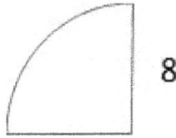

8

A.   Circumference of a circle is $2\pi r$, this is a quarter of a circle,

so the circumference would be $\frac{1}{4} * 2\pi r$.

$= \frac{\pi r}{2}$

$= \frac{\pi * 8}{2}$

$= 4\pi$

Thus, the total perimeter of the slice of pie is

$= 4\pi + 8 + 8$

$= 16 + 4\pi$ units.

240. Find the area of the sector of the circle?

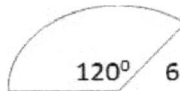

120^0 6

A.   *Note: the area of a sector of a circle is*

$\frac{1}{2}r^2\theta,$ *where θ is the angle of the sector in radians*

Here we have r = 6 and θ = 120°

Let us convert θ to radians = $120 * \frac{\pi}{180} = \frac{2\pi}{3}$ radians.

Thus, area of the sector is $\frac{1}{2}r^2\theta = \frac{1}{2}(6)^2 * \frac{2\pi}{3}$

= 12π sq units.

241. A restaurant offering smoothies offers them in three sizes tall, grande, and venti. They have apple, banana, peach, mango, and orange flavors and you can add Kale or protein enhancements for additional costs if desired. How many smoothie combinations are possible with one size, one flavor, and with or without Kale or protein enhancements or neither?

A. There are 5 different flavors, from which one is chosen in 5 different ways → (1)

There are 3 different sizes, from which one is chosen in 3 different ways → (2)

With Kale or protein enhancements, there are 2 different ways → (3)

Thus, combinations possible with one flavor, one size and either Kale or protein enhancements are obtained by multiplying (1), (2), and (3)

= 5 * 3 * 2

= 30 → (4)

The combinations possible with one flavor and one size, but neither Kale or protein enhancements are obtained by multiplying (1) and (2)

= 5 * 3

= 15 → (5)

Thus, the total combinations are the sum of (4) and (5)

$= 30 + 15$

$= 45.$

242. Find the number of triangles in the figure below?

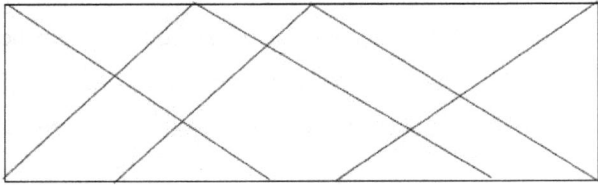

A.   Let's name the points to make it a bit easier:

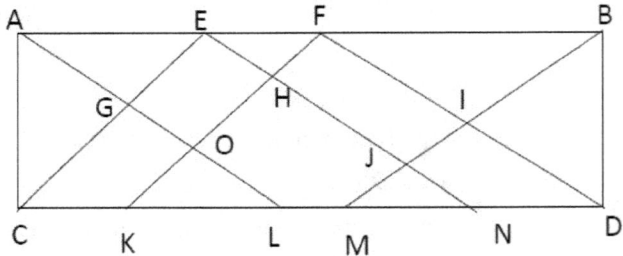

1.   ΔACL

2.   ΔAGC

3.   ΔAGE

4.   ΔAOF

5.   ΔBDM

6.   ΔBDI

7.   ΔBIF

8.   ΔBJE

9. ΔCGL

10. ΔCEN

11. ΔDIM

12. ΔDFK

13. ΔKOL

14. ΔKHN

15. ΔNJM

16. ΔEHF

17. ΔEAC

18. ΔFBD

Thus, we have 18 triangles.

243. Find the product of the distinct prime factors of 6592?

A. Let's find the factors of 3596 – starting with the smallest factors first

2|6592

2|3296

2|1648

2|824

2|412

2|206

103|103

|1

Thus, the distinct prime factors are 2 and 103.

The product of the prime factors is 2 * 103

= 206.

244. What is the lateral surface area of the cone below (let π = 3)

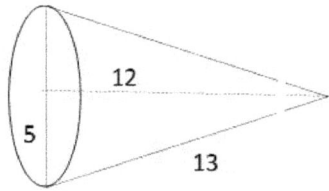

A.   Note: Lateral area of a cone is π * radius * slant height.

Here we have r = 5 and slant height = 13

= 3 * 5 * 13

= 195 unit^2.

245. What is the GCF of the monomials $m^7n^3o^3pq^4r^8$ and $n^8op^6q^4r$?

A.   GCF are the greatest common factors between

$m^7n^3o^3pq^4r^8$ and $n^8op^6q^4r$

= n^3opq^4r.

246. 20% of 300 is equal to 75% of a number. What is the number?

A.   Let n be the number.

20% of 300

= 0.2 * 300

= 60

Given, 75% of the number (n) is equal to 20% of 300.

75% * n = 60

$0.75n = 60$

n = 80.

247. $\cos\theta = \frac{1}{\sqrt{2}}$, find θ?

A. $\cos\theta = \frac{1}{\sqrt{2}}$

$\theta = \cos^{-1}(\frac{1}{\sqrt{2}})$

$\theta = 45°$.

248. Find the coordinates of the vertex of the quadratic equation $y = (x - 2)^2 - 6$?

A. *Note: For a quadratic equation $y = ax^2 + bx + c$, the x coordinate of the vertex is $-\frac{b}{2a}$, by substituting this x coordinate into the given equation, you get the y coordinate.*

Here the equation is,

$y = (x - 2)^2 + 6$

$y = x^2 - 4x + 4 + 6$

$y = x^2 - 4x + 10$ → (1)

So, here we have $a = 1$, $b = -4$, $c = 10$.

$x = -\frac{b}{2a}$

$x = -\frac{(-4)}{2*1}$

$x = 2$

Substituting value of x in (1) we get,

$y = (2)^2 - 4*2 + 10$

$y = 6$

Thus, the coordinates of the vertex are $(2, 6)$.

249. Find the value of n if 280 is the nth octagonal number?

A. *Note: The formula for nth octagonal number is $3n^2 - 2n$.*

So, here we have,

$3n^2 - 2n = 280$

$3n^2 - 2n - 280 = 0$

$3n^2 - 30n + 28n - 280 = 0$

$3n (n - 10) + 28 (n - 10) = 0$

$(3n + 28) (n - 10) = 0$

$n = -28/3$ or $n = 10$

n cannot be -28/3, so

n = 10.

250. John can mow his front yard in 15 minutes, while Amy can mow the same front yard in 20 minutes. If they work together, how long will it take for them to mow the front yard?

A. Let us find out the rate at which each of them can mow the yard.

John can mow the front yard in 15 minutes, so he mows $1/15^{th}$ of the yard in 1 minute → (1)

Amy can mow the front yard in 20 minutes, so she mows $1/20^{th}$ of the yard in 1 minute → (2)

So, together they can mow $(\frac{1}{15} + \frac{1}{20})$ of the yard in 1 minute

$= (\frac{1}{15} + \frac{1}{20})$

$= \frac{7}{60}^{th}$ of the yard in 1 minute

Thus, to mow the entire yard it will take $\frac{60}{7}$ minutes

= 8.6 minutes.

251. The sides of a triangle are 2a -1, a – 2, and 3a + 7. If the perimeter of the triangle is 46, what is the longest side?

A. The perimeter of the triangle is the sum of its sides.

2a - 1 + a – 2 + 3a + 7 = 46

6a + 4 = 46

a = 7

We know the largest side is going to be 3a + 7.

So, the length of the largest side is (3*7 + 7) = 28 units.

252. Find the lower boundary for the outliers in the box-whisker plot below:

```
        ┌──────────┬─────────────────────┐
   ─────┤          │                     ├─────
        └──────────┴─────────────────────┘
 ┬    ┬    ┬    ┬    ┬    ┬    ┬    ┬    ┬    ┬   ┬   ┬   ┬
28   30   32   34   36   38   40   42   44   46  48  50  52
```

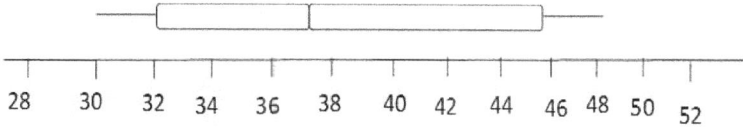

A. The median of the numbers 28, 30, 32, 34, 36, 38, 40, 42,
    44, 46, 48, 50, 52 is 40.

    The two sets of numbers on either side of the median are

    28, 30, 32, 34, 36, 38 → (1) and

    42, 44, 46, 48, 50, 52 → (2)

    Let's now find the median of these two sets

    The median of the set (1) which is 28, 30, 32, 34, 36, 38 is

    $\frac{(32+34)}{2} = 33$

    The median of the set (2) which is 42, 44, 46, 48, 50, 52 is

    $\frac{(46+48)}{2} = 47$

    Thus, the interquartile range (IQR) is the difference
    between these two medians

    $= 47 - 33$

    $= 14$

    Outliers are the points that are 1.5 times of IQR above and
    are below the two medians.

    So, the outliers are

    $33 - 1.5 * 14$

    $= 12$ → (3)

    and, $47 + 1.5 * 14$

    $= 68$ → (4)

    Then, the outliers are 12, 28 (the lowest number in the
    plot) and 68.

    The lowest outlier is 12.

253. What is the simple interest if you deposited $450 at a rate of $4 \frac{1}{8}$% for 72 months?

A. *Note: the simple interest per year is (principle * interest rate)/100*

   Here we have principle = $450 and interest rate = $4 \frac{1}{8}$%

   Thus, simple interest earned per year is

   $$= \left(\frac{450 * 4 \frac{1}{8}}{100}\right)$$

   $$= \left(\frac{300 * 9}{100 * 4}\right)$$

   = $18.56/year

   Now, 72 months = 72/12 = 6 years

   Thus, simple interest earned over 6 years is

   = 18.56 * 6

   = $111.38.

254. How many combinations can be made from 21 things taken 18 at a time?

A. *Note: the combinations of n things taken r at a time is*

   $$^nC_r = \frac{n!}{(n-r)!r!}$$

   Here we have n = 21 and r = 18

   $$^{21}C_{18} = \frac{21!}{(21-18)!18!}$$

   = 1330.

255. The sum of two numbers is 156 and their difference is 24. What is the remainder if the larger number is divided by the smaller number?

A. Let x and y be the two numbers.

   x + y = 156 → (1)

   x − y = 24 → (2)

   Solving for x, let us add (1) and (2)

$2x = 180$

$x = 90$

Substituting in (1) we get

$90 + y = 156$

$y = 66$

So, the two numbers are 90 and 66. When 90 is divided by 66, the remainder will be 24.

256. Find b:

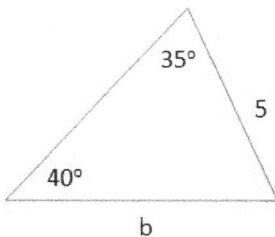

A. Applying the sine rule we have,

$$\frac{5}{sin40} = \frac{b}{sin35}$$

$b = \frac{5*sin35}{sin40}$

$b = 4.5.$

257. $3i^3(-4i + 2i^2)(i - 2i^4)$

A. We know that $i^2 = -1$ and $i^3 = -i \rightarrow$ (1)

Also, $i^4 = i^2 * i^2$

$= -1 * -1$

$i^4 = 1 \rightarrow$ (2)

Thus, using (1) and (2) we have,

$3i^3(-4i + 2i^2)(i - 2i^4)$

$= 3(-i)(-4i + 2(-1))(i - 2(1))$

$= -3i(-4i - 2)(i - 2)$

$= -3i(-4i^2 + 6i + 4)$

$$= -3i(-4(-1) + 6i + 4)$$

$$= -3i(4 + 6i + 4)$$

$$= -3i(8 + 6i).$$

258. Find n, if $\log_4 65536 = n$?

A. We know that if $\log_a b = c$, then $a^c = b$

Given, $\log_4 65536 = n$

Thus, $4^n = 65536$

$4^n = 4^8$

$n = 8$.

259. What is the area of regular octagon with a side length of 4 inches?

A. Note: Area of a regular octagon $= 2(1 + \sqrt{2}) * (side)^2$

Here side is 4 inches.

Thus, area of the octagon is

$$= 2(1 + \sqrt{2}) * (4)^2$$

$$= 32(1 + \sqrt{2}) \text{ inches}^2.$$

260. Simplify : $\left(-\dfrac{6a^3 b^{-2} c^5}{21 b^{-6} c^2}\right)^{-3} \div \dfrac{a^{-1} b^2}{a^4 c^3}$

A. $\left(-\dfrac{6a^3 b^{-2} c^5}{21 b^{-6} c^2}\right)^{-3} \div \dfrac{a^{-1} b^2}{a^4 c^3}$

$$= \left(-\dfrac{6a^3 b^{-2} c^5}{21 b^{-6} c^2}\right)^{-3} * \dfrac{a^4 c^3}{a^{-1} b^2}$$

$$= \left(-\dfrac{2a^3 b^4 c^3}{7}\right)^{-3} * a^5 b^{-2} c^3$$

$$= (-\dfrac{2^{-3} a^{-9} b^{-12} c^{-9}}{7^{-3}}) * a^5 b^{-2} c^3$$

$$= (-\dfrac{7^3 a^{-9} b^{-12} c^{-9}}{2^3}) * a^5 b^{-2} c^3$$

$$= (-\dfrac{343 a^{-9} b^{-12} c^{-9} a^5 b^{-2} c^3}{8})$$

$$= (-\frac{343a^{-4}b^{-14}c^{-6}}{8})$$

$$= -\frac{343}{8a^4b^{14}c^6}.$$

261. $(32_7 * 10_8) + (41_5 * 12_6) = -_7$

A.   Convert everything to base 10.

Let's take 32_7 and convert it to base 10.

$32_7 = 3 * 7^1 + 2 * 7^0 = 23 \rightarrow (1)$

Let's take 10_8 and convert it to base 10.

$10_8 = 1 * 8^1 + 0 * 8^0 = 8 \rightarrow (2)$

Let's take 41_5 and convert it to base 10.

$41_5 = 4 * 5^1 + 1 * 5^0 = 21 \rightarrow (3)$

Let's take 12_6 and convert it to base 10.

$12_6 = 1 * 6^1 + 2 * 6^0 = 8 \rightarrow (4)$

So, using (1), (2), (3) and (4) we have $(32_7 * 10_8) +$

$(41_5 * 12_6)$

$= (23 * 8) + (21 * 8)$

$= 352$

Now we have to convert this to base 7.

Step 1: Let us divide 352 by 7 to get the quotient and the remainder

7|352

|50 – quotient

We have 2 as the remainder (which cannot be further

divided by 7) $\rightarrow$ (5)

Step 2: Let us divide the quotient from step 1 which is 50

by 7 to get the quotient and the remainder

7|50

|7 – quotient

We have 1 as the remainder (which cannot be further divided by 7) → (6)

Step 3: Let us divide the quotient from step 2 which is 7 by 7 to get the quotient and the remainder

$$7 \rfloor 7$$

$$\lfloor 1$$

We have 0 as the remainder → (7)

Step 4: Let us divide the quotient from step 3 which is 1 by 7 to get the quotient and the remainder

$$7 \rfloor 1$$

We have 1 as the remainder (which cannot be further divided by 7) → (8)

Since we cannot divide this any further, we have everything that we need to convert 352 to base 7, we do this by using remainders from steps (5), (6), (7) and (8), but use them in the reverse order.

So, we take 2 from (5), 1 from (6). 0 from (7) and 1 from (8) and stack them in the reverse order by putting 1 from (8) first, followed by 0 from (7), followed by 1 from (6), and finally 2 from (5) to get 1012.

Thus, we have $352_{10} = 1012_7$.

262. A gear with 42 teeth makes 63 revolutions per min. It meshes with another gar that has 28 teeth. If the number of revolutions per min varies inversely to the number of teeth in a gear, what is the speed of the second gear in revolutions per min?

A. Since the speed varies inversely to the number of teeth we have,

$s = \frac{k}{t}$, where s is the speed in revolutions per min, k

is a constant and t are the number of teeth in the gear

→ (1)

We know that gear with 42 teeth makes 63

revolutions per min,

$63 = \frac{k}{42}$

k = 2646

Substituting in (1) we get,

$s = \frac{2646}{t}$

Thus, for the second gear with 28 teeth, the speed is,

$= \frac{2646}{28}$

= 94.5 revolutions per min.

263. If $f(x) = 4x^2 - (x-2)^2$, then find f(a + b)?

A. Given $f(x) = 4x^2 - (x-2)^2$

   $f(x) = 4x^2 - (x^2 - 2x + 4)$

   $f(x) = 3x^2 + 2x - 4$

   $f(a + b) = 3(a + b)^2 + 2(a + b) - 4$

   $= 3(a^2 + 2ab + b^2) + 2a + 2b - 4$

   $= 3a^2 + 6ab + 3b^2 + 2a + 2b - 4.$

264. Find the tens digit in 15^8?

A. *Note: The square of any number ending in a 5 has last two digits as 25.*

   Here we have 15^8

   $15^8 = 15^2 * 15^2 * 15^2 * 15^2$

   $15^2 = 225$, so all the numbers when multiplied will have 25 at the end.

Thus, the tens digit is going to be 2.

265. How many numbers greater than 0, but less than $(5^4 * 9)$ are relatively prime to $(5^4 * 9)$?

A. $(5^4 * 9) = 5625$

   The prime numbers that divide 5625 are:

   $5 \lfloor 5625$

   $5 \lfloor 1125$

   $5 \lfloor 225$

   $5 \lfloor 45$

   $3 \lfloor 9$

   $3 \lfloor 3$

   $\quad 1$

   Thus, the two unique prime numbers that divide 5625 are 3 and 5.

   The number of multiples of 3 that divide 5625 are $5625/3$ = 1875.

   The number of multiples of 5 that divide 5625 are $5625/5$ = 1125.

   The number of multiples of (3*5) that divide 5625 are $5625/15 = 375$.

   The positive numbers less than 5625 that are relatively prime to 5625 are,

   = 5625 - (1875 + 1125 - 375)

   = 3000.

266. Find the measure in radians of the reference angle of $\frac{3\pi}{5}$ radians?

A. *Note: to convert radians to degrees we multiply by* $\frac{180}{\pi}$.

Here we have $\frac{3\pi}{5}$, so let's convert this to degrees

$= \frac{3\pi}{5} * \frac{180}{\pi}$

$= 108°$

Note, reference angle is the smallest acute angle formed by the line with the x-axis (horizontal). It can be positive or negative.

Thus, the reference angle (smallest acute angle) formed by $\angle A$ is

$= 180 - 108$

$= 72°$

Note: to convert degrees to radians we multiply by $\frac{\pi}{180}$.

$=72 * \frac{\pi}{180}$

$= \frac{2\pi}{5}$ radians.

267. For $x \geq -5$, simplify: $\sqrt{9x^5 - 45x^4} + \sqrt{4x^5 - 20x^4} - \sqrt{12x^5 - 60x^4}$

A. $\sqrt{9x^5 - 45x^4} + \sqrt{4x^5 - 20x^4} - \sqrt{12x^5 - 60x^4}$

$= \sqrt{9x^4(x - 5)} + \sqrt{4x^4(x - 5)} - \sqrt{12x^4(x - 5)}$

$= 3x^2\sqrt{(x - 5)} + 2x^2\sqrt{(x - 5)} - 2\sqrt{3}x^2\sqrt{(x - 5)}$

$= (5 - 2\sqrt{3})\, x^2\sqrt{x - 5}$

268. Determine the domain of the square-root function $y = \frac{3}{5}\sqrt{3x - 7.5} + 8$

A. *Note: the domain of a square-root function is found by placing the expression inside the square-root as greater and equal to zero.*

We have $y = \frac{3}{5}\sqrt{3x - 7.5} + 8$

Let us place the expression inside the square-root as greater than and equal to zero.

$3x - 7.5 \geq 0$

$3x \geq 7.5$

$x \geq 2.5$.

269. What is the area of the triangle below?

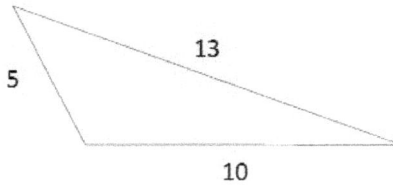

A. *Note: Area of a triangle given the three sides a, b, and c is*

$$\sqrt{p(p-a)(p-b)(p-c)}$$

where $p = \frac{a+b+c}{2}$.

Here we have a = 5, b = 10, and c = 13.

Perimeter p $= \frac{5+10+13}{2} = 14$

Thus, Area $= \sqrt{p(p-a)(p-b)(p-c)}$

$= \sqrt{14(14-5)(14-10)(14-13)}$

$= 6\sqrt{14}$ sq. units.

270. Let $\angle A = 27°36'52"$ and $\angle B = 42°54'14"$. What is $\angle A + \angle B$ in DMS form?

A. DMS is degree-minutes-seconds format.

Let us start off by adding the seconds first

$= 52 + 14$

$= 66"$

$= 1'6" \rightarrow (1)$

Let us now add the minutes

$= 36 + 54$

$= 90'$

$= 1°30' \rightarrow (2)$

Let us now add the degrees

$= 27 + 42$

$= 69° \rightarrow (3)$

We now add the corresponding degrees, minutes, and
    seconds from (1), (2) and (3)

$= 70°31'6''.$

271. What is the equation of a tangent that touches the circle at
    (2, -4) and the equation of the circle is $(x + 2)^2 + (y - 3)^2 = 25$?

A.   *Note: The equation of a circle in standard form is $(x - h)^2 + (y - k)^2 = r^2$.*

     Here (h, k) are the coordinates of the center and r is the radius of the circle.

     Given that the equation of the circle is $(x + 2)^2 + (y - 3)^2 = 25$, so the coordinates of the center of the circle are (-2, 3).

     We know that the segment from the center of the circle to point where the tangent touches the circle is perpendicular to the tangent.

     Let us find the slope of the segment that passes center of the circle and touches the tangent – it has coordinates (-2, 3) and (2, -4)

     Note: Slope of a segment with end points (x_1, y_1) and (x_2, y_2) is:

     $$\frac{y_1 - y_2}{x_1 - x_2}$$

141

Here the coordinates are (-2, 3) and (2, -4)

$$= \frac{3-(-4)}{-2-2}$$

$$= -\frac{7}{4}$$

We know that the product of the slope of the tangent and slope of this segment needs to be -1, so the slope of the tangent is $\frac{4}{7}$.

The equation of a line is given by,

$y - y_1 = m(x - x_1)$ where m is the slope and (x_1, y_1) is the point on the line.

Thus, the equation of the tangent with slope $\frac{4}{7}$ and passing through (2, -4) is

$$y - (-4) = \frac{4}{7}(x - 2)$$

$$7y + 28 = 4x - 8$$

$$y = \frac{4}{7}x - \frac{36}{7}.$$

272. If we roll a dice and toss a coin, what is the probability of getting a head and an odd number?

A. There are six outcomes when we roll a dice, the odd outcomes are 1, 3 and 5. Thus, the probability of getting an odd number after rolling a dice is,

$$= \frac{3}{6}$$

$$= \frac{1}{2} \rightarrow (1)$$

There are two outcomes when we toss a coin. Thus, the probability of getting a head after tossing a coin is,

$$= \frac{1}{2} \rightarrow (2)$$

Thus, the probability of getting an odd number after rolling a dice and getting head after tossing the coin is obtained by multiplying (1) and (2)

$$= \frac{1}{2} * \frac{1}{2}$$

$$= \frac{1}{4}.$$

273. Don has 6 shirts and 8 pants. How many days can he go without new clothes if wants to wear a different pant and shirt combination each day?

A. Don can wear a combination of a different shirt and pant each day for,

$$= 6 * 8$$

$$= 48 \text{ days.}$$

274. If there are equal number of girls and boys trying to get on a golf team. The golf team needs to have 6 people. How many different formations of the team are possible if you need at least 4 girls on the team and there are 5 girls trying out.

A. Since there are equal number of boys and girls trying out, the number of boys trying out is also 5. So there will be 5 boys and 5 girls trying out. There are two combinations possible for the team:

Combo 1.   4 girls and 2 boys

Combo 2.   5 girls and 1 boy

So, for Combo 1 we need to choose 4 girls out of 5 and 2 boys out of 5, so we have $^5C_4 * {}^5C_2 = \frac{5!}{4!(5-4)!} * \frac{5!}{2!(5-2)!}$

$= 50 \rightarrow (1)$

And for Combo 2 we need to choose 5 girls out of 5 - that will only happen one way as we have 5 girls and we will choose all 5 of these girls. To choose 1 boy out of 5,

so we have $^5C_1 = \dfrac{5!}{1!(5-1)!}$

$= 5 \rightarrow (2)$

Thus, the total formations of the team are obtained by

adding (1) and (2) = 50 + 5 = 55 ways.

275. Find x if $\log_3 2187 - \log_3 9 = \log_4 x$

A. We know that $\log_m a - \log_m b = \log_m \dfrac{a}{b}$

Thus, $\log_3 2187 - \log_3 9$

$= \log_3 \dfrac{2187}{9}$

$= \log_3 243$

$= \log_3 3^5$

$= 5 \rightarrow (1)$

Given $\log_3 2187 - \log_3 9 = \log_4 x$, so substituting (1) we get,

$\log_4 x = 5$

$x = 4^5$

$x = 1024.$

276. A pouch contains 5 green, 7 red and 8 violet balls. Find the number of red balls that need to be added to the pouch, so that the probability of drawing a red ball is ¾?

A. Let x be the number of additional red balls.

The total red balls would be 7 + x.

The total balls in the pouch would be

$5 + 7 + x + 8$

$= 20 + x$

The probability of drawing a red ball from the pouch is,

$= \dfrac{7+x}{20+x}$

Given that the probability of drawing a red ball is ¾

So, we have

$$\frac{7+x}{20+x} = \frac{3}{4}$$

$28 + 4x = 60 + 3x$

$x = 32$

Thus 32 red balls will need to be added to the pouch.

Ordering Form

School/Teacher/Individual Name:

_____

School/Individual Address: _____

_____

City: _____State: _____

Zip: _____ Country: _____

Number of copies requested: _____

Pricing Information:

1-5 Copies: $10.99/copy

6-10 Copies: $9.99/copy

11-20 Copies: $8.99/copy

20+ Copies: $7.99/copy

Please add $3.99 for standard shipping & handling or $6.70 for 2-day priority shipping. Please send an e-mail if you need other faster delivery options.

Please make check payable to: **SAMIKA KULKARNI**

Payment or Ordering Form Mailing Address:

520 E VINE ST # 709

KELLER, TX 76248

For bulk orders, discounts, urgent orders, online payments, online book download, feedback, and/or questions, please contact competemath@gmail.com.

www.ingramcontent.com/pod-product-compliance
Lightning Source LLC
Chambersburg PA
CBHW060259050426
42448CB00009B/1694